Into the Gale

12 Evangelistic Lessons
from the Book of Acts

Larry Stamm

© 2018 by Larry Stamm

All rights reserved. No part of this publication may be reproduced, stored in a retrieval system, or transmitted in any form or by any means without the prior written permission of the author. Exceptions are made for brief quotations used in printed interviews.

Cover design by Ken Raney (kenraney.com)

Bible quotations are from the New King James Version (NKJV) unless otherwise marked. New King James Bible © 1979, 1980, 1982, Thomas Nelson, Inc.

Other verses are drawn from the New American Stand Bible (NASB) © 1960, 1971, 1973, 1975, 1977, 1995 by the Lockman Foundation. The Holy Bible: English Standard Version (ESV). Wheaton: Standard Bible Society, © 2016.

1st Edition

Also By Larry Stamm

Serving In His Court:
Biblical Principles For Personal Evangelism From The Heart Of A Coach'

Print and audio formats available at larrystamm.org
Kindle version available at Amazon.com

Acknowledgements

First and foremost, I want to thank my Lord and Savior Jesus, who is my life and in whom I live, breathe and have my being. A huge thank you goes out to my beautiful and supportive wife Lori. In addition to being my partner in life and best friend, she's also my greatest champion and partner in ministry. Many thanks to Alton Gansky, my editor; Ken Raney, my graphic artist; and Jack Cavanaugh, my interior page designer. Their professional expertise and support were tremendous and helped make this project possible. A big thank you goes out to Tim, Bryan, Benjamin, and Barbara for their various contributions to this book. Finally, to the many people and churches who've sown into my spiritual life throughout the years, thank you for investing in me and in eternity.

Table of Contents

Preface	9
Introduction	13
Chapter 1— The Engine That Powers Our Witness	23
Chapter 2— All For One	33
Chapter 3— The Clash	47
Chapter 4— Friends Not Foes	59
Chapter 5— A Surprising Catalyst	75
Chapter 6— Navigating Cultural Waters	85
Chapter 7— Picking Your Battles	101
Chapter 8— God Gives The Increase	111
Chapter 9— Interruption And Opportunity	125
Chapter 10— Mighty In The Scriptures	135
Chapter 11— Trial And Testimony	147
Chapter 12— Out Of The Doldrums And Into The Gale	161
About The Author	171
Connect With Larry	177
Endnotes	179

Preface

"For the times they are a-changin . . ." Familiar words. Words penned over fifty years ago by musician Bob Dylan. The title song is one of the most iconic of the 1960s and became an anthem for many in that unsettled period of US history. Dylan called it "a song with a purpose." It was meant to be more than entertaining. The tumultuous '60s included such cultural and societal tsunamis as the civil rights movement, the Vietnam war, and the sexual revolution.

Fast forward a little over fifty years later to this day and we all can understand the statement, "Oh, the times, they are still a a-changin!" Can I get an amen?

We can point to some obvious current flash points of change: the technological revolution, political chaos and pandemonium, or the battle over gender identity.

There is another social tsunami that has arisen in recent years, a massive change that is germane to our walk with Christ and our witness for Him. What is it? It is a wind of change that blows against the church in America, affecting all believers: increasing persecution of God's people.

Wind. It affects all of our lives, some more than others. But make no mistake, wind, though invisible, is real. We may not see wind, but its effects are obvious.

Wind can be cataclysmic or catalytic, depending on how it blows and how it is utilized. Sometimes wind is out of control and devastating as in a hurricane or tornado. Other times, it is pleasant, useful, and welcomed, like a cool breeze in the summer.

Growing up on the west coast of Florida in the Tampa Bay area, I was keenly aware of the wind. I would regularly go sailing with my father and I learned to respect the wind. Wind is the power that fills the sails and propels the vessel through the water. In fact, a good strong wind (but not too strong) is preferable. However, in sailing, too much wind is undesirable. If the wind is blowing high enough, then it may be dangerous to raise the sails, or even be in the open water at all. Growing up on the Gulf Coast makes one attune to the fact that hurricanes are an annual threat with devastating winds.

It goes without saying, but tropical storm or hurricane conditions will keep a sailing vessel in a harbor. However, there are times when the weather, unpredictable as it sometimes can be, may sneak up and wreak unexpected havoc on a sailor in open water.

When I was around ten-years-old I was with my father and several other people on a morning sail on Tampa Bay. Tampa Bay can be volatile. It has earned the name, "Lightning Capital of the World." Meteorologists measure lightning strikes around the world, and on a certain year, Tampa Bay has recorded more bolts than anywhere else on the planet.

On this fateful morning, we were sailing on his 39-foot Trimaran—a sailboat with one larger center hull and two outer smaller hulls. It was a very stable boat. Yet, on this occasion, the weather rocked it.

We only had the main sail up on that morning because the wind was quite brisk. Then, seemingly out of nowhere, there was a loud boom. In a split second, the mast, which holds the mainsail in place, was on the deck. Miraculously, no one on board was hurt. It turned out we hit, or rather, we were hit by a white squall.

A white squall is a sudden and violent windstorm not accompanied by the black clouds generally characteristic of a squall. On this morning, while there were some dark clouds in the sky, there was no sign of a squall line heading our way. This white squall came out of nowhere.

Wind. Mysterious in some ways, yet real and powerful. Depending on the situation and activity, the wind can work for or against us.

In the spiritual world, wind is an essential component in the Christian life. Jesus used the metaphor of wind to describe the Christian life:

"Most assuredly, I say to you, unless one is born of water and the Spirit, he cannot enter the kingdom of God. That which is born of the flesh is flesh, and that which is born of the Spirit is spirit. Do not marvel that I said to you, 'You must be born again.' The wind blows where it wishes, and you hear the sound of it, but cannot tell where it comes from and where it goes. So is everyone who is born of the Spirit" (John 3:5-8).

In the Hebrew, *spirit* is the word *ruach*, meaning wind. The *Holy Spirit* in Hebrew is *Ruach HaKadosh*—HaKadosh meaning *holy*,

So, in one sense, the literal movement of our Christian life is affected by the impact of the Spirit. This is exciting, powerful, and in some ways, mysterious. Yes, the impact of the Spirit is evident.

What also is evident is that in the spiritual realm there are winds that oppose our witness as followers of Jesus Christ. Those headwinds are opposition, hostility, and persecution.

For our purposes, I'll wrap up those three terms into the word *persecution*.

What is persecution? Theologian Geoffrey Bromily's definition is excellent: "Persecution is the suffering or pressure, mental, moral, or physical which authorities, individuals, or crowds inflict on others, especially for opinions or beliefs, with a view to their subjection by recantation, silencing, or, as a last resort, execution." [1]

Pastor, author, and former President of Moody Bible Institute, Paul Nyquist, in his tremendous book, *Prepare—Living Your Faith in an Increasingly Hostile Culture*, states: "Persecution is the societal marginalization of believers with a view to eliminating their voice and influence." [2]

Persecution has a goal: To silence our voice and eliminate our influence.

Persecution doesn't want God's people to follow the Lord, to walk in the light and proclaim the gospel. Persecution doesn't want us to proclaim, "Jesus died for our sins according to the Scriptures, was buried and rose again on the third day according to the Scriptures" (1 Corinthians 15:3-4). And persecution doesn't want us to communicate to people that through faith in Christ, they can be forgiven of their sins, be reconciled to God and experience the abundant and eternal life the Lord promised to those who trust in Him.

The winds of persecution are gaining strength here in the United States. And though not a white squall in a spiritual sense, it's part of an overall storm that appears to be growing in intensity daily.

In our nation's history, the church has undoubtedly been blessed in unique ways. Our nation was built upon Judeo-Christian values. This foundation has provided unique freedoms and privileges for God's people. You might say the church in America operated for much of our history in an environment of smooth sailing.

And yet, today, at seemingly blinding speed, many rights, privileges, and blessings afforded believers in America are shrinking, or are being attacked and challenged.

Many Christians are dismayed by the changing spiritual current blowing across the land. What once was a tailwind that aided the effort of the American church in fulfilling the Great Commission has become a headwind that grows stronger.

In light of the increasing opposition, hostility, and persecution to believers in America today—to borrow a phrase from Francis Schaeffer—we ask, "How then shall we live?"[3] And if we use the wind analogy we ask, "How then shall we sail into the gale?"

Do we shrink up, give up, or give in to those who would silence our Christian testimony? Or is there another response to that increasing tempest blowing against us?

This book is a simple response to the increasing spiritual headwinds we as the church in America are facing. Come aboard, and let's take a ride, keeping our eyes on Jesus, the "captain of our salvation" (Hebrews 2:10).

Introduction

"Every knock is a boost," boasted Moishe Rosen, the founder of the Jews for Jesus ministry, an organization with which I served for eight years. This memorable phrase is a reminder of the catalytic affect of persecution. When you're a Jewish Christian serving as a missionary to your fellow Jews, telling them Jesus is the Messiah, God in the flesh, and Savior of the world, there will be a strong response. I had to be prepared for strong, sometimes negative reactions—many of which were unpleasant.

Each time I received a negative reaction, I reminded myself of Moishe Rosen's words: "Every knock is a boost." My experiences reminded me of the polarizing nature of the gospel message, the spiritual war I was in, and that I was on the right track. This is nothing new. It is part of the very fabric of church history. The testimonies of the Apostle Paul, the other apostles, and first century believers also evoked a strong response. There was opposition, hostility, and physical persecution. That hasn't changed in 2000 years. This knocking of our faith need not be catastrophic. It can be a catalyst. A catalyst is a substance that brings about a reaction but is not changed in the process. That's the scientific definition. In life, a catalyst is a person or event that changes things. That's what the Gospel does. It changes things. It changes people.

The challenge for the American church is acknowledging the changing cultural tide of our country. Our nation is moving away from our Judeo-Christian moorings. For nearly 250 years, believers in the United States were able to live in freedom and with little persecution. Society supported and promoted biblical values. Today, our moral free fall from biblical values is, like a receding tide, moving us into uncharted waters.

A healthy perspective acknowledges that historically, persecution of Christians has been a global norm. While at the same time, the

American church has inhabited a safe port of sorts. Today, with increasing speed, as storm clouds of persecution and winds of change blow, our anchor is being raised and we are drifting into the open ocean, experiencing more of what our brethren worldwide have experienced—persecution becoming the norm and less the exception.

You might say, the open ocean and exposure to all its dangerous elements, including the gale of persecution, is our new normal. We have left the safe harbor of our past and are entering a whole new season. And yet, God remains the same and the Great Commission is still our mandate.

So, how then shall we live?

For first century believers, persecution certainly was catalytic. It didn't engulf them, it galvanized them; it unified them; it crystalized the importance of their mission; it focused them; and it motivated them—the spiritual war Jesus predicted had become a reality.

For example, when the believers were run out of Jerusalem as recorded in Acts 8, their forced move turned into a means of spreading the gospel. That knock served as a boost.

This book is about our response to the rising persecution against the American church. Our being knocked may be catalytic, not catastrophic, in our efforts to fulfill the Great Commission.

Personal Experience Of The Gale

A gale is a very strong wind. We've noted wind as it pertains to sailing and the spiritual realm. When we look at the present culture war we see a spiritual gale blowing directly against the church in America—a gale that seeks to discourage, dissuade, demean and diminish our witness.

I've experienced the gale in my faith journey, both personally and in Christian vocational ministry.

Being a Jewish believer in Jesus and the first Christian in my family, my father disowned me in 1992. I came to the Lord in late 1987, but I spent the first eighteen months as a "closet Christian." It took that long to share my faith with my entire family.

The last two people I shared with during that season of life were my father and my paternal grandmother—his mom. Having shared my faith in Jesus with my dad, he told me that was fine. He even said he was happy for me. Then he told me to never share my faith with my grandmother. Shortly thereafter, I did share my faith with her. And although she didn't understand, she was happy for me. This began a deterioration in my relationship with my father that culminated in him cutting off all contact with me. We never spoke again. He died in 2012.

I became a vocational missionary working in New York City from 2003-2009. I have experienced the sting of persecution, hostility, and opposition to my faith. Having shared my faith in Messiah Jesus on the streets of the Big Apple and other major cities around the world, I have been kicked, spit at, threatened and called every name in the book—even some names not in the book.

Even in my personal life, I have been shunned, avoided, and have felt the pressure to remain silent.

Gale Force Rising

For most of our nation's grand history, a nation built upon Judeo-Christian values, we've been rather insulated from the wind. It's been smooth sailing. But the winds of change have risen, and they are not friendly to the cause of Christ.

For context, here's a tremendous working definition of culture by Ifte Choudhury:

> Culture is a way of life for a group of people—the behaviors, beliefs, values and symbols that they accept, generally, without thinking about them, and that are passed along by communication and imitation from one generation to the next.[4]

Simply put: a culture is how and why people do things. Culture is complex and includes all human actions and institutions, such as entertainment, the arts, education, religion, law, morality, technology, and economic activity. At the same time, while culture is complex, it's also dynamic and ever-changing.

This volume is not a study of culture or our culture wars specifically. If you're a believer in America, this cultural conflict between the secular and sacred (Christianity in particular) is evident. And with this simple, yet important understanding, we strive to learn how to be salt and light amid an increasingly corrupt and perverse generation. For as our culture moves away from a Judeo-Christian foundation, it becomes increasingly hostile to the church.

I don't know your Christian experience, but if you are living in America—you no doubt are aware of the persecution that is growing in intensity. The present gale blowing against our Christian witness began swirling in the tumultuous and turbulent 1960s.

These landmark Supreme Court decisions are illustrative of the growing gale assaulting the church:

- The attack against the Bible and prayer. The Supreme Court—in a series of three decisions in 1962 and 1963—removed the Bible and prayer from our public schools.

- The attack on life. The destructive *Roe v Wade* Supreme Court ruling in 1973, legalizing abortion, is responsible for the death of over 55 million human lives, while harming millions of women and men whose "choice" has caused death, regret, and shame.

- The attack on the family. The Supreme Court's decision to redefine marriage in 2015, made gay marriage the law of the land and placed it on the same footing as traditional marriage. The family is the fundamental building block of all human civilizations., and marriage—the marriage between a man and woman—is the foundation of the family.

Additionally, the gale is not only institutional, it's personal, as these recent headlines illustrate:

- "Air Force Veteran Faces A Court Martial For Opposing Gay Marriage," John Hawkins; townhall.com; Sep 17, 2013

- "Court: Christian Baker Must Provide Wedding Cakes for Same-Sex Couples," Todd Starnes, FoxNews.com; August 13, 2015
- "Christian Nurse Fired for Offering Prayer Before Surgery," wnd.com Dec. 12, 2016

James Emory White articulates well the gale that blows in America today:

> Compared to the violence against Christians in many places around the world, the answer is no. Christians in America experience nothing compared to the persecution of Christians in such places as Nigeria, Iran, Pakistan, Egypt or Syria.
>
> What is happening in America is an increasing hostility and intolerance toward Christian beliefs and values that many perceive to be an attack on religious freedom. In current American culture, you are free to be a Christian as long as you don't actually live out your faith, vote your faith, take a stand in relation to your faith, or believe others should embrace your faith.
>
> In other words, it can be privately engaging, but must remain socially irrelevant. [5]

But there's more.

A real concern is the growing insistence that faith be private has now become a demand for faith to be compromised. It's not enough that your beliefs can't influence society; you must also embrace society's beliefs. As Jonah Goldberg noted in USA Today, the opposition to many Christian values has become an "if you're not with us, you're against us" mentality." [6]

In so many words, "Christians beware." In contrast, we need to be aware, awaken to, and enter this reality—being the salt and light that God calls us to be—in face of the gale.

In the last fifty plus years we could also highlight the rise of postmodernism, secularism, humanism, and in recent years a rise in what some call "militant atheism," a worldview that is ardent in its effort to stamp out all things religious, including Christianity.

Yes, the gale is growing in strength and the American church is standing directly in its crosshairs. This trend is troubling and discouraging, but it is our reality. And what do we do with such circumstances? Will we seek shelter or fight the good fight? Will we walk in fear or walk by faith?

Nothing New Under The Sun

Although the rising spiritual headwinds in America may appear relatively recent, the dynamic is nothing new for the church. In fact, Jesus taught His first followers they would experience the gale of opposition, persecution and hostility.

For example, He said, "Remember the word that I said to you, "The servant is not greater than his lord." If they have persecuted me, they will also persecute you" (John 15:20). The Lord also stated, "And you will be hated by everyone because of My name" (Luke 21:17).

Two-thousand years later, the church is still opposed by the world. Two-thousand years later, God is still moving mightily through His people. Yes, Jesus is building His church and "the gates of Hades shall not prevail against it" (Matthew 16:18).

In fact, headlines from the first century church would read like today's, both negatively and positively.

Negative Headlines:

- "Believers Beaten and Threatened for Speaking the name of Jesus" (Acts 4).

- "Follower of Jesus stoned to death following public sermon" (Acts 7).

- "Christians kicked out of Jerusalem" (Acts 8).

- "Well-known Missionary On Trial For Evangelism Activities" (Acts 22-26).

Positive Headlines:
- "New Religious Movement Exploding Despite Intense Opposition" (Acts 9).
- "Jewish Sect Reaching Out To Gentiles With Message Of Faith, Hope, and Love" (Acts 11-15).
- "Jesus Followers Committed And United Amidst Persecution" (Acts 11).
- "Believer in Jesus says people's salvation more important than His safety" (Acts 22-26).

Amidst the gale, Jesus' words from the Sermon on the Mount did and still should greatly encourage His people: "Blessed are you when they revile and persecute you, and say all kinds of evil against you falsely for My sake. Rejoice and be exceedingly glad, for great is your reward in heaven, for so they persecuted the prophets who were before you" (Matthew 5:11-12).

I would be remiss not to mention that the spiritual gale that opposes our Christian testimony is only part of the narrative—a challenging part. What we need to keep front and center in our minds is that we have the wind of the Holy Spirit, who propels us forward. So be encouraged.

When we walk by faith, we walk in the power of the Holy Spirit, and in Him is victory—"For whatever is born of God overcomes the world. And this is the victory that has overcome the world—our faith" (1 John 5:4).

Ancient Example, Contemporary Application

This project flows from a series of weekly evangelistically-oriented, online devotions I wrote in 2015 and 2016. I took my inspiration directly from the book of Acts.

I undertook writing this book to encourage and inspire believers in the United States to fight the good fight of faith, specifically in our personal evangelistic efforts—by understanding and applying foundational principles found in the book of Acts.

Why Acts? First and foremost, because this powerful New Testament book chronicles the birth and expansion of the early church. As we'll see, for our first century brothers and sisters, following Jesus was difficult and dangerous. At the same time, this challenging context for ministry was not catastrophic. Rather, in many ways, it was catalytic. And this is the thesis for our brief study.

Acts is a historical book about early Christian missionary work. The key word in the book is *witness*, which is found twenty times. As such, the bent of this book leans toward our becoming effective witnesses as we press on in the faith into the gale. With this in mind, Acts 1:8 is perhaps the key verse from the entire book of Acts. And my hope is that through the power of the Holy Spirit, the Lord will use this book as a tool in growing your witness for His glory. This book is not academic—it's practical. The lessons elucidated herein are meant to be understood, internalized and applied to our daily witness.

And this book is certainly not exhaustive—we're only briefly touching upon twelve important principles I trust the Lord will use to inspire, instruct, and perhaps challenge you to be more intentional in your Christian walk, and in your personal witness to others.

This book will not chronicle the culture wars. There are many tremendous works on that topic written by people much smarter and more well-equipped than me. Rather, I hope you'll simply see our current context for ministry is not much different than it was for our first century brethren—the gale of persecution is blowing. Humanly speaking, they faced stormy waters. But the difficulty and challenges they faced were in many ways catalytic, not catastrophic.

Yes, our historical bubble here in America has burst to some degree. And humanly speaking, this is not desirable. Yet in the spiritual realm, it may be a catalyst for a healthy environment in a new season of growth for God's people. I pray we would grow—in trusting

God, in trusting in each other, and becoming a more distinct light for Christ in the midst of a an increasingly corrupt and perverse generation.

Yes, the gale is growing. The power of God's Spirit is also blowing. Still, we remember that "He who is in us is greater than he who is in the world" (1 John 4:4).

My hope is that these twelve lessons will provide instruction, inspiration and will help us grow, for "faith comes by hearing and hearing by the Word of God" (Romans 10:17). Ultimately, I hope these lessons will encourage and equip you to be a more effective witness for Jesus. Sharing our faith is the one thing we can't do in heaven. Additionally, I pray that this study will entice you into a deeper study of the book of Acts and the Word of God in general.

May this book be an encouragement, exhortation, inspiration, and a challenge to God's people here and elsewhere. May we see our emerging cultural context as an opportunity, not an obstacle. How? By walking by faith, not sight—while fixing our eyes on Jesus, the author and finisher of our faith.

I once heard someone say, "You don't choose your reality. You do choose to enter your reality."

May these lessons instruct and inspire us to faithfully enter our present reality and fulfill the Great Commission...for Jesus' glory and for the building of His church.

Chapter 1

The Engine That Powers Our Witness

Wind is power. Since early recorded history, people have harnessed the energy of the wind. In my youth, I experienced this powerful influence sailing with my father. "In the ancient world, wind energy propelled boats along the Nile River as early as 5000 B.C. By 200 B.C., simple windmills in China were pumping water, while vertical-axis windmills with woven reed sails were grinding grain in Persia and the Middle East.

New ways of using the energy of the wind eventually spread around the world. By the eleventh century, people in the Middle East used windmills extensively for food production. Returning merchants carried this idea back to Europe. The Dutch refined the windmill and adapted it for draining lakes and marshes in the Rhine River Delta. When settlers took this technology to the New World in the late nineteenth century, they began using windmills to pump water for farms and ranches and later to generate electricity for homes and industry." [7]

"The first electricity-generating wind turbine was a battery charging machine installed in July 1887." [8]

"Later, the twentieth century electricity-generating wind turbines developed and were utilized around the world. The force of the wind makes the wind turbine blades spin, and the energy of this motion is converted into electricity by a generator." [9]

Obviously, without wind, those turbines would be useless. But in utilizing the wind, these turbines are quite useful. Interestingly, these turbines work just fine in high winds—even gale force winds.

In the spiritual realm, just as turbines harvest the winds of nature, we as believers are called to access the wind of the Spirit, the Holy Spirit, in our walk with the Lord.

Jesus made comparisons between the wind and the Holy Spirit. He said, "The wind blows where it wishes, and you hear the sound of it, but cannot tell where it comes from and where it goes. So is everyone who is born of the Spirit" (John 3:8).

And when the Holy Spirit fell upon and filled the disciples at Pentecost in Acts 2, He was described this way: "And suddenly there came a sound from heaven, as of a rushing mighty wind, and it filled the whole house where they were sitting" (Acts 2:2). This was not a weather phenomenon, rather a supernatural event. In Hebrew and Greek, the words for wind and spirit are synonymous. Wind is frequently used as a picture of the Spirit (cf. Ezekiel 37:9).

Just as the building of the turbine is man's initiative to harness the power of the wind to create electricity, so you and I must be intentional in accessing the power of God, namely the Holy Spirit, in becoming powerful and effective witnesses for Him.

And how do we access this power? Faith.

Interestingly, wind energy is a free, renewable resource. Its use does not affect its future supply.

In the spiritual world, our access to the Holy Spirit is unlimited. He is always in us and ready to empower us. We are called to "walk in the Spirit" (Galatians 5:16) and "be filled by the Spirit" (Ephesians 5:18). This means we surrender to the Lord in faith, being obedient to His Word and following where He leads.

The Holy Spirit powers our walk and witness. Without His power, we will be spiritually unplugged. Apart from the Holy Spirit guiding, leading, and empowering us, our ability to witness is incapacitated. No power. No effectiveness. No fruit. And although we may be able to perform the mechanics of the Christian life, including the work of evangelism, in our natural strength, without God's power its end is fruitless. Jesus said in John 15:5, "Without Me you can do nothing." The Psalmist wrote, "Unless the Lord builds the house, they labor in vain who build it" (Psalm 127:1).

Jesus said to His disciples just before He ascended into heaven: "But you shall receive power when the Holy Spirit has come upon you; and you shall be witnesses to Me in Jerusalem, and in all Judea and Samaria, and to the end of the earth" (Acts 1:8).

Acts 1:8 is a key verse in the entire book of Acts. It contains the disciple's mission and power source to accomplish that mission—the person of the Holy Spirit.

Ten days after Jesus gave that directive, the Spirit did fall on the disciples at Pentecost (the Jewish feast of Shavuot), and the disciples were off and running. Three thousand people were saved that day and the movement expanded just as the Lord had promised. Just as His promises and His power were critical to the effort of His people in the first century, so they are for us today.

In fact, the Holy Spirit is the lead actor in the book of Acts. Not only was He the wind that powered the turbines of the early church, He is also the engine that powers our witness today as we press on into the gale. To paraphrase Paul: "For we can do all things" [that bear fruit and have real spiritual impact] through Christ, who strengthens us" (Philippians 4:13). Therefore, we need to stay connected to the source.

Power translates from the Greek word *dunamis*, from which we get the word "dynamite." Every believer contains the spiritual dynamite he or she needs for the Christian life, including an empowered witness. In short, the Holy Spirit is to our witness what physical wind is to wind turbines—it's the source—the essential source of energy.

Jesus taught the apostles by the Holy Spirit, who was both the source and power of His ministry (Matt. 4:1, 12:18, 28; Mark 1:12, Luke 3:22, 4:1, 14, 18). And upon tasking them with the Great Commission, the Lord promised the Holy Spirit would be their ministry power.

We can't overstate the importance of the Holy Spirit's work in and through us, as well as in the hearts of those we seek to reach. He is the one who transforms the human life. Therefore, we will continue to refer to His character and work throughout this book.

So, while the gale of growing persecution moves against us, the wind of the Spirit propels us forward into the gale, for His glory, our good, and for the blessing of those to whom we minister.

Going Where No Man Has Gone Before

As we think about the gale of persecution that seeks to impede us, let's acknowledge real barriers that must be crossed in order to accomplish the Great Commission. When Jesus said, "Go and make disciples of all nations," He reminded the disciples that He would be with them always, through the person of the Spirit:

> And Jesus came and spoke to them, saying, "All authority has been given to Me in heaven and on earth. Go therefore and make disciples of all the nations, baptizing them in the name of the Father and of the Son and of the Holy Spirit, teaching them to observe all things that I have commanded you; and lo, I am with you always, even to the end of the age." Amen. (Matthew 28:18-20).

Imagine being a disciple and hearing Jesus' command to "make disciples of all nations" and His prediction that they would be His witnesses to the "ends of the earth." That must have been an incredible shock.

There would be barriers to bridge and lines to cross. How could they understand that command? By faith in the one Who would never leave them or forsake them. And not only faith in Him, but faith in His promised empowerment to engage and fulfill the mission.

Where We Go...In His Power

By its very nature, the Great Commission requires faith. How was that original band of Jewish misfits going to go out and share the Jewish Messiah with the nations of the world...with people so different from them? In the book of Acts, as it is for us today, there were massive challenges to be met. In the face of these challenges, we note astounding and inspiring demonstrations of faith and of the Spirit's power.

There were established religious lines to be crossed. In Acts 2–4 there was teaching, preaching, and healing happening in Jesus' name. The only problem was the Jewish religious establishment. Religious leaders had resisted, rejected, and ultimately persecuted Jesus to the point of death. They carried that hatred to the disciples and the early church. It was Jesus' followers who were emphatically crossing the lines of appropriate religious decorum—doing all of it in His name and in His power.

In Acts 2, after the Spirit came at Pentecost, Peter preached to the Jewish crowd and, as already mentioned, 3000 people responded to the Gospel. In Acts 3-4, after Peter and John had healed a lame man in Acts 3, they were arrested by the religious leadership (the Sanhedrin) and asked by what power or name had brought about the miracle. Peter, "being filled with the Holy Spirit," stated:

> "Rulers of the people and elders of Israel: If we this day are judged for a good deed done to a helpless man, by what means he has been made well, let it be known to you all, and to all the people of Israel, that by the name of Jesus Christ of Nazareth, whom you crucified, whom God raised from the dead, by Him this man stands here before you whole" (Acts 4:8-10).

While we applaud the boldness, courage, and faith of Peter and John, we need to remember these were the same disciples that had fled in fear when Jesus was taken and crucified. Now, we see them not only crossing the line, but also disregarding the potential personal consequence of crossing that line. And how did they do it? Through the power of the Holy Spirit.

Today, we're told by the politically-correct (PC) crowd that religion is fine, as long as it's private. "Don't make waves," they say.

"Don't speak. Don't proselytize." The religious barrier in the first century was the Jewish establishment. In the first century, as noted, it pressured the Messianic Jewish believers not to teach or heal "In His Name" (Acts 4:18).

Today, the religious lines are drawn. Warnings not to cross these PC-constructed lines include pressure from various political and social groups who desire to make the expression of our faith strictly private. If it's private, the establishment tells us, it's okay. But once you go public, you've crossed the line. And chronicling current Christian persecution here in America is difficult, because it's so rampant. One simply need to do an Internet search for "Christian persecution in America" to get the idea—"Don't cross the line, or there will be trouble."

There are cultural bridges to be crossed. When Jesus told the disciples they'd be His witnesses "in Jerusalem, and in all Judea and Samaria, and to the end of the earth" (Acts 1:8), "Jerusalem and Judea" would be right up their alley, while the words "Samaria" and "to the ends of the earth" would have shaken them—it was beyond their imagination.

Being His witnesses in Jerusalem and Judea would be understandable, as the disciples would have been comfortable on some level with this very familiar territory. They'd spent three and a half-years in the "Jesus School of Ministry," which by the way, was organic, intensely personal, and practical. In short, it was real–life unplugged. And for the most part, it took place in their familiar territory, Jerusalem and Judea. So, the locale for being His witnesses on their home turf of Jerusalem and Judea on the surface wouldn't provide such a challenge.

What would present a great challenge would be Samaria. Why? Because Samaria was a place of division, acrimony, and polarization. Jewish people typically wouldn't step into Samaria. They viewed Samaritans with disdain. The Assyrians invaded and exiled the Northern Kingdom of Israel seven centuries earlier. It was their practice to subject people through intermarriage, taking away their ethnic distinction. Jews from the conquered Northern Kingdom intermarried with Assyrians creating a new people group called Samaritans. Jews from the south, Judea, would later see the Samaritans as half-breeds, and held them in contempt. As you might imagine, Samaritans didn't take kindly to such vitriol and developed a mutual disdain for their critics.

If going to Samaria wasn't bad enough, Jesus was sending them to the "end of the earth." By faith, the Lord would call them to places they did not know, much the same as He called Abraham to go to a land "God would show him" (Genesis 12:1).

Jesus had given them a glimpse of cross-cultural ministry when He ministered to the Samaritan woman at the well in John 4. Here, the disciples got a preview of ministering outside their comfort zone.

In Acts 10, the Lord called Peter to preach the gospel to Cornelius—a Gentile—and his entire household. The Jewish people's disdain for Samaritans paled in comparison to their hatred of Gentiles (non-Jewish people). Some Jewish people had nothing to do with Gentiles, not open to hosting or being hosted. In fact, dirt from a Gentile country was considered defiled to certain religious Jewish people, and some would shake it off their sandals before entering Israel.

In this context, Peter is called to not only enter the home of Cornelius, but eat food that wasn't kosher and share the good news about the Jewish Messiah. That required faith and the power of the Holy Spirit.

Part of our call as Jesus-followers today is to cross cultural bridges, bringing the truth and grace of God to places and to people different than we are.

Today, we don't need to leave our country to cross cultural bridges. Our ever-increasing diversity means the Lord may call us to reach out to Muslims, atheists, homosexuals and irreligious in our own country.

And though our world screams of political correctness, divisiveness, and built-in barriers, the Lord commands us to, cross the line, smashing barriers to reach those precious souls in need of salvation.

And how will this happen? We walk by faith in the power of the Holy Spirit.

The increasingly diverse US population also demands that we not avoid those who are different, even those who push back against us. Instead we lean against the gale, against the forces crying out, "Stay back," and reach out to them.

And how are we going to do it? The same way the early disciples did. We plug into the Source, depend on Him in all ways. We must fight the good fight of faith against built-in polarization for the sake of the ministry of reconciliation (2 Corinthians 5:18-19), which God has entrusted to us.

What We Do…In His power

The Holy Spirit gives us boldness. After Peter and John had healed a lame man in Acts 3, they were arrested by the Jewish religious leadership and asked by what power or name they had done it. Peter, "being filled with the Holy Spirit," then witnessed to them, saying in Acts 4:12, "Salvation is found in no one else, for there is no other name under heaven given among men by which we must be saved."

Peter and John saying Jesus was the only way to be saved among the religious establishment was admirable, compelling, controversial and courageous. You and I proclaim the exclusivity of Jesus in salvation to a post-modern, pluralistic, and divided culture and that takes the same kind of boldness God gave those disciples.

The Holy Spirit helps us know what to say. In Luke 12:12 (also Matthew 10:18-20), Jesus was teaching the disciples not to fret about what they might say when undergoing persecution, telling them "the Holy Spirit will teach you in that very hour what you ought to say." In our witnessing efforts, we should strive to "always be ready" (1 Peter 3:15) to share when God provides opportunities. We need to also trust in the power of the Spirit to know when and what to share. And

God is faithful.

The Holy Spirit does the work of conviction, righteousness, and judgement: As we boldly go in His power, proclaiming "the truth that sets men free" (John 8:32), the Holy Spirit is working and moving in people's lives. Just before Jesus was crucified, He shared the following words with the disciples in the Upper Room: "Nevertheless I tell you the truth. It is to your advantage that I go away; for if I do not go away, the Helper will not come to you; but if I depart, I will send Him to you. And when He has come, He will convict the world of sin, and of righteousness, and of judgment" (John 16:7-8).

I Don't Have The Gift..Just The Power

I personally don't have the spiritual gift of evangelism. What about you? But I do know we are all called to be witnesses for Jesus. If you're a Jesus-follower, you have the Holy Spirit, the engine that powers your witness. And the one thing we all need to power that engine? Faith.

Remember the first disciples were of no great pedigree. Jesus didn't choose the best and brightest, those with the gift of evangelism, to be His witnesses. Rather their gifting was in the person, power, and presence of God. He was their gift (2 Corinthians 9:15). In fact, when the Sanhedrin "perceived that they were uneducated and untrained men, they marveled. And they realized that they had been with Jesus" (Acts 4:13).

And therein lies the key for us as we strive to be powerful witnesses. Spend time with the Lord. Spend time in His Word. And spend time in prayer. Remember, a powerful witness is a "plugged-in" witness—for it is the Holy Spirit Who is the wind that powers the turbine of our witness.

I can tell you that I desperately need the Holy Spirit in my personal witness to others. I need Him to fill me, to empower me, to help me know what to say, and to give me courage to cross lines, cross bridges, and connect with people in our ever- changing cultural context—all for Jesus' sake and for His glory. How about you?

Chapter 2

All For One

"The Volvo Ocean Race, the premier yacht race around the world, is held every three years. The event began in 1972 when England's Whitbread company and the British Royal Naval Sailing Association agreed to sponsor a globe-circling regatta, which would be called the "Whitbread Round the World Yacht Race."

The nine-month long event, usually beginning in October, consists of nine or ten legs. Crews must prepare to sail day and night, around the clock, for weeks on end, until a leg or portion of the race is complete. Some individual legs of the race require more than twenty days to complete." [10]

Winning the race does not attract a cash prize, as the feat of competing is presented as sufficient reward. "There is no prize money for winning the Volvo Ocean Race—just the prestige of overcoming one of the greatest challenges in professional sport." [11]

Sailing a vessel in the ocean for extended periods of time exposes the boat and crew to potential severe meteorological phenomena. "The worst weather conditions during the Volvo Ocean Race usually occur in the Southern Ocean where waves sometimes top 100 feet and gusts can reach seventy miles-per-hour." [12]

As you might imagine, heading across open waters with one goal in mind—completing the leg at hand, and ultimately the race—requires commitment, dedication, and unity. Whatever weather conditions arise, there is no turning back. The team must face any and all weather conditions—be they ideal or severe—together.

The crew must be united in effort, purpose, and vision to successfully deal with any eventualities the sea can bring. They must maintain an "All for one" attitude—the one being the race.

Our race is the Great Commission. And rather than a nine month around-the-world endeavor, ours is a 24/7 task that continues until Jesus returns or takes us home. In addition, our race requires us to fulfill our individual roles and work synergistically with others on our racing team, the church, to fulfill the Great Commission. We must work together as a team amid the tempest of opposition—we must be all for one.

We would do well to understand the increasing gale of opposition to our faith. As we seek to serve the Lord, and share Him with others, we have a choice to make. We can ignore or try to avoid dealing with our reality, or we can lean into that reality.

We need not fear, shun, or avoid the challenges to the Great Commission today. Rather, we must face them together, being unified in our task.

Establishing And Maintaining Unity

When Jesus told his followers in Matthew 28, "Go out and make disciples of all nations," they were to go out in one accord, unified in effort and purpose.

Also, while Jesus was giving His final marching orders just before His arrest and crucifixion in what we know commonly as the "Upper Room Discourse," He said:

"By this all will know that you are My disciples, if you have love for one another" (John 13:35).

Here we get a hint into the upcoming corporate witness of the believing community of Jesus-followers. One of the distinguishing characteristics of their witness to the world would simply be their love for one another. Simple, yes. Profound, yes. Easy...not so much.

And two thousand years later we can identify. Can I get an amen?

Jesus knew a community united would be powerful and effective, a community divided weak and ineffective.

I have witnessed this reality in my own Christian experience. Thinking back to the 1990's just before entering full-time vocational Christian work for the first time, a good friend gave me forewarning.

He said, "Larry, the most difficult thing about ministry will not be your outreach, it will be getting along with your co-laborers." And I have learned, over and over again—sometimes painfully so—that a house divided cannot stand. Perhaps you've also experienced this as you've sought to function in a local church family or ministry organization. But a house united is powerful. And I have also experienced this wonderful and power-packed dynamic in my walk with God. The power behind that unity is love, the love of God expressed through the power of the Holy Spirit—"the love of God has been poured out in our hearts by the Holy Spirit who was given to us" (Romans 5:5).

When the church is born in Acts 2, we see 3000 people baptized on the day of Pentecost (Acts 2:41). Immediately following, we see the power and effectiveness of a united church:

> "And they continued steadfastly in the apostles' doctrine and fellowship, in the breaking of bread, and in prayers. Then fear came upon every soul, and many wonders and signs were done through the apostles. Now all who believed were together, and had all things in common, and sold their possessions and goods, and divided them among all, as anyone had need. So continuing daily with one accord in the temple, and breaking bread from house to house, they ate their food with gladness and simplicity of heart, praising God and having favor with all the people. And the Lord added to the church daily those who were being saved" (Acts 2:42-47).

It is challenging to comprehend the love these early believers had for one another, because in our contemporary church, we're not of "one accord." We see the standard and should strive to "do life together," loving one another. And for what purpose?

That they may know.

"They" refers to those who've not yet met the Savior. It seems to me our saltiness and brightness (Matthew 5:13-16) is somewhat connected to our love for one another. And yes, as individuals we strive to be salt and light. Our saltiness and brightness also contains a corporate component because you and I are part of one body—called the church (1 Corinthians 12:14-31).

The body of Christ will most effectively function when moving in a coordinated effort—that effort being driven again by love. Interestingly, the Apostle Paul shows the way of love in the "love chapter" (1 Corinthians 13), which cuts to the core of the matter of love:

Love suffers long and is kind; love does not envy; love does not parade itself, is not puffed up; does not behave rudely, does not seek its own, is not provoked, thinks no evil; does not rejoice in iniquity, but rejoices in the truth; bears all things, believes all things, hopes all things, endures all things. Love never fails (1 Corinthians 13:4-8).

And this love applies not only to our outreach as God's people, it involves our "in-reach."

In Acts 2 that corporate witness of the church characterized by love was incredibly powerful and attractive. The effect of that loving community of faith resulted in the church finding "favor with all the people" and "the Lord adding to the church daily those who were being saved" (Acts 2:47).

The Power of Love for us is to live out the Sweet Song of Salvation—united, engaged, and committed to the effort of the church—that unbelievers may come to know Christ. This thrust is characterized by love and the first example of this corporate love and witness is seen in Acts 2.

What does it mean for you and me to fulfill this command to "love one another?" That is a matter of prayer. It certainly looks different in application for each of us, but the principles are overarching as we see.

May we grow in our love for one another, that they may know we are His disciples—to the end that some would come to know Jesus personally. Amen.

Identifying Conditions Opposing Our Unity

Just as sailors need to be aware of changing weather conditions affecting their ability to function during a race such as the Volvo Oceans Race, we as God's people need also to be aware of those conditions capable of opposing our unity as the church.

First and foremost, we understand our American culture is moving away from biblical values, and as such, is blowing against those of us who stand for the truth, as we've discussed this earlier in our study.

But there are two other points of opposition working against our effort in maintaining biblical unity as God's people I want to introduce in this chapter. They are critical to understand as we navigate these stormy waters. They are the denominational divide and satanic opposition. But, before we go there, first a lesson from our first century brethren that will inform our effort in maintaining unity today as God's people.

Issues Affecting The Unity Of The Early Church

As twenty-first century American Christians, we comprise an assortment of denominations with their associated beliefs and expressions of the faith.

Denominations help people distinguish theological differences. Those differences can also be a source of divisiveness and arrogance, pitting one group against another.

In Matthew 16:18, Jesus said, "I will build My church, and the gates of Hades shall not prevail against it."

David Pratt wrote: "The Gospel records that He built one church and that all saved people were in that church. He prayed for unity and rebuked division." [13] In 1 Corinthians 1:10, the Apostle Paul pleaded, "[Let] there be no divisions among you." Even back then there were divisions that threatened the unity of the early church.

In the first century church there was a major internal conflict, not denominational in nature, but cultural. And this cultural conflict threatened the unity and ultimately the effectiveness of God's people to carry out the Great Commission. For our purposes I will call it the "Jewish-Gentile Divide."

Here's the setting: As we've mentioned already, in Acts 10 God commanded the Apostle Peter to go to Cornelius' house and preach the gospel. Cornelius is Gentile. This would make any Jew pause and Peter was no different. Add to that, God also told Peter to eat food that wasn't kosher. At first glance, Cornelius hearing the gospel may seem like a small detail. But in fact, for a Jewish man, not only was eating "traif" (non kosher food) a big deal, but connecting on any level with a Gentile was a cultural affront to Peter's upbringing.

Try and understand Peter's situation. The challenge he faced two-thousand years ago is not so different from the challenge we face today. In the first century, there was a cultural divide between Peter and Cornelius—between Jew and Gentile.

First century Jews would generally have nothing to do with Gentiles. This separation began in the Old Testament. God told Israel, "be holy as I am holy" (Leviticus 11:44). Part of that holiness was separation from Gentile nations. Why? Gentiles worshipped false gods and practiced pagan religions. Individual Gentiles who became converts or proselytes to Judaism in the Old Testament had restrictions. Even in the Temple that God Himself designed and Solomon built, there was the Court of Gentiles— an area where Gentile converts were permitted provided they conducted themselves in a reverent manner. They were never allowed beyond that point. The rest of the Temple area was reserved for Jews.

Unfortunately, as time passed, pride, prejudice, and a superior attitude based upon this difference caused many in the Jewish community to consider themselves superior to Gentiles. First century Jews would never be guests in Gentile homes or invite Gentiles into theirs. As mentioned a little earlier, dirt from a Gentile country was considered defiled and a Jewish person would shake it off his sandals before entering Israel (that's where we get the expression "shake the dust off"). Also, Jews would not eat food prepared by Gentile hands. In short, Gentiles were considered unclean and their presence defiling. You get the idea.

Put yourself in Peter's sandals for a moment. You are a Jewish believer in Y'shua (Jesus) the Jewish Messiah, the "Consolation of Israel" (Luke 2:25). In addition, Jewish believers were initially considered just another sect of Judaism. Cornelius threw the proverbial "monkey wrench" into the mix. Being a Roman military officer would have also made Cornelius an affront to many in the Jewish community. He represented the Roman Empire in the first century, a foreign force that occupied the land and oppressed the Jews.

Considering all this, we must ask: who or what could possibly bridge this cultural divide? Jesus and His message of salvation could.

Peter went to Cornelius' home and said: "You know how unlawful it is for a Jewish man to keep company with or go to one of another nation. But God has shown me that I should not call any man common or unclean. Therefore I came without objection as soon as I was sent for. I ask, then, for what reason have you sent for me?" (Acts 10:28-29).

Cornelius revealed how God told him in a vision to summon Peter to come to his home. Then he said they were ready to hear what God had commanded Peter to share. Peter shared the gospel, adding:

> "Of him (Jesus) all the prophets bear witness that through His name everyone who believes in Him receives the forgiveness of sins."
>
> While Peter was still speaking these words the Holy Spirit fell upon all those who were listening to the message. All the circumcised believers (Jewish believers) who came with Peter were amazed, because the gift of the Holy Spirit had been poured out on the Gentiles also" (Acts 10:43-44 NASB).

Yes they were amazed. This was God's plan from the beginning.

Remember God's covenant He made with Abraham. He told Abraham that through him, all the nations of the world would be blessed (Genesis 12:1-3). And God provided clues about His plans for the nations in many Old Testament prophecies, including Isaiah 49:6, where God states His plan for Gentile salvation,

He says, "It is too small a thing that You should be My Servant
To raise up the tribes of Jacob and to restore the preserved ones of Israel;
I will also make You a light of the nations
So that My salvation may reach to the end of the earth" (NASB).

Peter and the others were witnessing Bible prophecy come alive before their very eyes.

After Cornelius and his household came to faith, many Gentiles are brought into the church. At the same time, many Jewish believers don't quite understand and need this new reality explained. Then in Acts 11, Peter is confronted by fellow Jews regarding Gentile conversion, "Peter, are you sure this Gentile thing is kosher?" And Peter told them, "God said it was okay for Gentiles to be for Jesus." After Peter tells them the story of Cornelius, the other disciples begin to understand. Their response is found in Acts 11:18, "Well then, God has granted to the Gentiles also the repentance that leads to life" (NASB).

Following this scene, we find Gentiles flooding into the church in great numbers (Acts 12-14). And by the time we get to Acts 15, there arises a new divisive conflict caused by Gentile salvation.

The new conflict centered on the following question: Did Gentiles have to follow the Jewish custom of circumcision and follow the law of Moses to be saved? After Paul and Barnabas report on Gentile conversion, some believers raise the issue: "But some of the sect of the Pharisees who believed rose up, saying, "It is necessary to circumcise them, and to command them to keep the law of Moses." Now the apostles and elders came together to consider this matter" (Acts 15:5-6).

Peter cuts to the heart of the matter: "So God, who knows the heart, acknowledged them by giving them the Holy Spirit, just as He did to us, and made no distinction between us and them, purifying their hearts by faith. Now therefore, why do you test God by putting a yoke on the neck of the disciples which neither our fathers nor we were able to bear? But we believe that through the grace of the Lord

Jesus Christ we shall be saved in the same manner as they" (Acts 15:8-11).

Unity was found at the heart of the matter—salvation is found by grace alone through faith alone in Christ alone—regardless of whether a person is Jewish or Gentile. Divide presented. Divide successfully crossed. And that lesson of keeping the main thing the main thing sets a good example for us today as we face a huge threat to unity within our community—a spiritual gale warning.

Overcoming The Twenty-First Century Denominational Divide

We've illustrated a major first century point of division that threatened church unity. And we've noted our twenty-first century denominational construct as a threat to unity in the American church.

My purpose is not to endorse or condemn the present denominational structure, but rather to point out the obvious need and lay a framework for finding biblical unity.

Biblical unity will make the church stronger and our efforts more effective as we seek to run the race set before us—the race believers have been called to run.

In the first century church, the New Testament had not yet been penned. What unified the church doctrinally was a collection of core beliefs commonly known as the Apostle's Creed:

> I believe in God, the Father Almighty, Maker of heaven and earth. And in Jesus Christ, His only begotten Son, our Lord; who was conceived of the Holy Spirit, born of the virgin Mary; suffered under Pontius Pilate; was crucified, dead, and buried; He descended into hell; The third day He arose again from the dead; He ascended into heaven and sitteth at the right hand of God the Father Almighty; from there He shall come to judge the living and the dead. I believe in the Holy Spirit. I believe a holy catholic [universal] Church, the communion of saints; the forgiveness of sins; the resurrection of the body; and life everlasting. Amen. [14]

Short. Poignant. Powerful. These beliefs provided the foundation of Christian doctrine the church agreed on. And with agreement, came unity.

But what of our twenty-first century threats to unity which denominationalism brings?

Certainly there are no simple answers. Yet our foundation for unity should be in the authority of God's Word, and core teachings found therein.

Seventeenth century German Lutheran theologian Rupertus Meldenius wrote, "In essentials, unity; in non-essentials, liberty; in all things, charity."[15] Today the phrase is well-known and has been attributed to other theologians like Augustine. And for good reason - it packs a punch!

In their excellent book *Conviction Without Compromise*, authors Ron Rhodes and Norman Geisler lay out a helpful list of what the essentials include:

God's Unity; God's Tri-unity; Christ's Deity; Christ's Humanity; Human Depravity; Christ's Virgin Birth; Christ's Sinlessness; Christ's Atoning Death; The Bodily Resurrection of Christ; The Necessity of Grace; The Necessity of Faith; The Bodily Ascension of Christ; Christ's Priestly Intercession ; Christ's Bodily Second Coming; The Inspiration of Scripture; and The Literal Interpretation of Scripture.[16]

Now, these are the hills to die on, where we contend for the faith. These are non-negotiable. If we don't have unity of belief here, we don't have true Christian unity. For example, we must agree Jesus is God. If not, we can't have biblical unity. We also must believe in the literal resurrection of Christ. If not, then we don't have biblical unity.

Then there are non-essentials, where liberty is found. In those non-essentials, unity may be preserved even where different beliefs abound. Non-essentials include views on end-times, forms of church government, the nature and function of communion, and use of musical instruments in worship.

In short, when it comes to Christian unity, which is critical as we seek to fulfill the Great Commission, we must major on the majors, and keep the main things the main things, all according to God's

Word.

The Apostle Paul exhorted the Ephesian church to be united:

> "I, therefore, the prisoner of the Lord, beseech you to walk worthy of the calling with which you were called, with all lowliness and gentleness, with longsuffering, bearing with one another in love, endeavoring to keep the unity of the Spirit in the bond of peace. There is one body and one Spirit, just as you were called in one hope of your calling; one Lord, one faith, one baptism; one God and Father of all, who is above all, and through all, and in you all" (Ephesians 4:1–6).

As God's people, we need to stand strong in the core—in what unifies us. And that unity must be found first and foremost in those biblical essentials. And when we are united here, we are a crew that can face with power and effectiveness whatever the sea of our culture can throw at us.

As we strive for biblical unity, may the Lord grant us the wisdom to discern essential and non-essential doctrine, that we may preserve true Christian unity as He would desire.

Our True Enemy

The war waged against us from the outside emanates from the devil and his minions. As Christian writer Mark Howell, notes, "When you declare you allegiance to Jesus Christ, you declare war on hell. When you declare war on hell, hell puts up a fight."[17] 1 Peter 5:8 states, "Be sober, be vigilant; because your adversary the devil walks about like a roaring lion, seeking whom he may devour."

Paul made a similar warning: "For we do not wrestle against flesh and blood, but against the rulers of the darkness of this age, against spiritual hosts of wickedness in the heavenly places" (Ephesians 6:12).

The enemy of our souls will do anything and everything within his power to keep us from being the unified people of God, reaching out to a lost and dying world.

People, who make up the foundation of our culture, are not the enemy. Remember, Satan influences our culture and the people living in it, "But even if our gospel is veiled, it is veiled to those who are perishing, whose minds the god of this age has blinded, who do not believe, lest the light of the gospel of the glory of Christ, who is the image of God, should shine on them" (2 Corinthians 4:3-4).

The devil's strategy of opposing our Christian life is referred to by the Apostle Paul in Ephesians 6:11 as "wiles of the devil." In our ecclesiastical efforts, he seeks to render the church less effective in a variety of ways, but to divide and conquer is one way of disrupting Christian unity and its associated power and effectiveness.

Jesus stated in Matthew 12:25, "Every kingdom divided against itself is brought to desolation, and every city or house divided against itself will not stand."

There's more to be said regarding satanic opposition to our unity and our effort to effectively live out the Great Commission, which we'll see in future chapters. For now, we note the obvious: Satan and his minions oppose the unity of our faith community, and as such, also opposes our effort in fulfilling our Great Commission mandate.

Jesus: The Last Word On Unity

It was Jesus' final Passover meal, the last time He would celebrate it with His disciples. It was here He instituted communion. And it was here He uttered his final words to them prior to His crucifixion. In John 17, as part of what's commonly known as the Upper Room Discourse, Jesus provides instruction to and prayer for His disciples. But he also, in a few poignant verses, prays for future believers—that would be you and me.

And part of that prayer is a petition for unity to exist among God's people:

> "I do not pray for these alone, but also for those who will believe in Me through their word; that they all may be one, as You, Father, are in Me, and I in You; that they also may be one in Us, that the world may believe that You sent Me" (John 17:20-21).

The Lord prayed that His church, would "be one," as the Father and Son were one (John 10:30). Now that's unity. This oneness or unity included not only our communion with God, but our relationship with one another.

Matthew Henry summarized well our "oneness" with each other:

> That they might all be knit together in the bond of love and charity, all of one heart. That they all may be one, (1.) In judgment and sentiment; not in every little thing—this is neither possible nor needful, but in the great things of God (2.) In disposition and inclination. All that are sanctified have the same divine nature and image; they have all a new heart, and it is one heart. (3.) They are all one in their designs and aims. Every true Christian, as far as he is so, eyes the glory of God as his highest end, and the glory of heaven as his chief good. (4.) All one in love and affection. Every true Christian has that in him which inclines him to love all true Christians as such." [18]

What is the purpose of this unity? That the world may believe. There is a correlation between oneness of the church and "wonness" of the world to Christ. So, yes, our unity with each other impacts our testimony to others.

Remember, biblical unity as we've framed it is based on the essential doctrines we noted earlier. Based on that standard, how unified are you with Christians of different beliefs, who otherwise hold to those same essentials? Do you avoid the brethren whose different views are mainly peripheral and non-essential Christian doctrines? If so, what difference do you think it would make in your personal walk to work at seeking unity where unity can be found? These are issues, again, to take up with the Lord. He desires that we be united with Him and each other.

May we as God's people face the gale opposing our unity, in its varied forms, and strive for unity where unity can be found. And when we're pulling together, working together amidst the storms of life, we will be closer to our God, each other, and will be more effective in our witness to others.

Lord, help us through the power of Your Spirit, to fight the good fight in maintaining unity whenever possible, to finish the course—together as Your church—and to keep the faith. Amen.

Chapter 3

The Clash

Growing up in Florida, I spent considerable time outdoors. Whether sailing or playing tennis, I was always looking up to the sky, cognizant of weather conditions. I was fascinated with weather.

My interest moved me to take a meteorology class in college. You might say I was taken by weather. I would have liked to be one of those on-location weathermen—you know, the guys in the midst of the hurricane or massive snowstorm. Fun, exhilarating, and perilous stuff.

Spending time outdoors in Florida, one must be aware of violent weather, mainly severe thunderstorms. They can spring up quickly and be dangerous. And speaking of spring, across our great country, the USA's most violent weather usually occurs during spring when continental polar air clashes with maritime tropical air. When the two collide along what is known as a frontal boundary, which separates air masses, an explosion of energy can ensue, causing violent and sometimes deadly weather. Tornadoes, damaging winds, severe thunderstorms, snow, and hail all make up the potpourri of climatic chaos and pandemonium.

At the turn of the twentieth century weather fronts had yet to be identified and categorized. Today forecasters casually talk about "cold fronts" and "warm fronts." The lines on the weather map are familiar to us all. But where did the term "front" come from?

"Back in 1900, weather maps used an "H" to indicate the center of a high-pressure area, L's for centers of low pressure, and lines of equal pressure (isobars) drawn around the highs and lows. Warm fronts and cold fronts were absent. Meteorologists hadn't discovered them yet.

In 1919, Norwegian meteorologist, Wilhelm Bjerknes of the Bergen School of Meteorology, conceived the notion of fronts: air masses clashing along a boundary. He named these boundaries "fronts" after the battlefronts of WWI." [19]

Invisible physical phenomenon, air masses colliding and manifesting severe weather is one thing. But in the spiritual life there is another kind of collision creating polarization, persecution, and conflict. It is the collision of light and darkness. And when spiritual light collides with spiritual darkness, there's a reaction and response, sometimes a violent one.

Jesus describes the reason for such polarization: "He who is not with Me is against Me" (Matthew 12:30, Luke 11:23). The battle lines have been established, the spiritual frontal boundaries, have been drawn—by the Lord Himself. The clash of light and darkness is inevitable and quite evident today. Our first century brethren also encountered the clash. From them we can learn valuable lessons about the clash and how to walk in the light amid the whirlwind that occurs when darkness is exposed by light.

The Clash Of Light And Darkness

I like to experience thunder storms, particularly at night. Lightning has an unparalleled capacity to engage the night and expose things normally shrouded in darkness. This exposure is remarkable.

Spiritual light is also quite amazing, revealing both truth and exposing darkness. And in the spiritual, whenever light exposes darkness, there is a reaction and a response.

There is a dramatic example of this in Acts 3. Peter and John are approaching the temple when they encounter a lame man begging for alms (Acts 3:1-3):

> And fixing his eyes on him, with John, Peter said, "Look at us." So he gave them his attention, expecting to receive something from them. Then Peter said, "Silver and gold I do not have, but what I do have I give you: In the name of Jesus Christ of Nazareth, rise up and walk." And he took him by the right

hand and lifted him up, and immediately his feet and ankle bones received strength. So he, leaping up, stood and walked and entered the temple with them—walking, leaping, and praising God. And all the people saw him walking and praising God. Then they knew that it was he who sat begging alms at the Beautiful Gate of the temple; and they were filled with wonder and amazement at what had happened to him (Acts 3:4-10).

How is a man lame his entire life healed in a flash? It was by the same power that controls the clouds and makes the lightning—the power of God (Job 37:11,15; Matthew 8:23-27).

When the religious leaders questioned him about the healing, Peter explained:

> "Men of Israel, why do you marvel at this? Or why look so intently at us, as though by our own power or godliness we had made this man walk? . . . And His name, through faith in His name, has made this man strong, whom you see and know. Yes, the faith which comes through Him has given him this perfect soundness in the presence of you all" (Acts 3:12, 16).

Peter goes on to proclaim the gospel (Acts 3:17-26) to this captivated audience. In one sense, you would think this miraculous work would result in unanimous approval. A lame man healed—this is awesome, right? Well, not so fast. This miracle was done in Jesus' name, and the name above all names creates a reaction and response unlike any other name.

The spiritual light of the gospel brings revelation and conviction, resulting in salvation for some. For others, this revelation and conviction results in rejection and even vehement opposition to the light:

> Now as they spoke to the people, the priests, the captain of the temple, and the Sadducees came upon them, being greatly disturbed that they taught the people and preached in Jesus the resurrection from the dead. And they laid hands on them, and

put them in jail until the next day, for it was already evening. However, many of those who heard the word believed; and the number of the men came to be about five thousand (Acts 4:1-4).

It was not the miracle that offended the religious leadership. It was the message behind the miracle, and more specifically, the name behind the message—Jesus. Jesus is at the core of the gospel message. He is the rock of salvation that leads to liberation and life for those who believe. But for those who oppose and reject Jesus, He is a rock of offense that leads to condemnation and judgement (1 Peter 2:8).

This is the clash of light and darkness.

Following Jesus is to walk in the light:

Then Jesus spoke to them again, saying, "I am the light of the world. He who follows Me shall not walk in darkness, but have the light of life" (John 8:12).

Rejecting Jesus is to continue in darkness:

"And this is the condemnation, that the light has come into the world, and men loved darkness rather than light, because their deeds were evil. For everyone practicing evil hates the light and does not come to the light, lest his deeds should be exposed. But he who does the truth comes to the light, that his deeds may be clearly seen, that they have been done in God" (John 3:19-21).

As you live for the Lord and seek to shine the light of Christ, understand the clash. Expect the clash, and forge on in spite of it. Remember, while many will run from the light, some will walk into the light and be saved. Hallelujah! Either way, if you're living for the Lord, you are going to be a lightning rod.

"For you were once darkness, but now you are light in the Lord. Walk as children of light (for the fruit of the Spirit is in all goodness, righteousness, and truth), finding out what is acceptable to the Lord. And have no fellowship with the unfruitful works of darkness, but rather expose them" (Ephesians 5:8-11).

Facing The Tempest Of Opposition

"You have to tell your family you believe in Jesus," he exclaimed. These were not words I wanted to hear. They startled, shook, and challenged me. And yet, this charge was the will of God.

It was late December 1987, and I had just came to faith in Jesus a few weeks earlier. I was on the phone with my good friend Greg, who had been a key witness for Christ to me during my college years.

Being Jewish and believing in Jesus has its challenges. To add, I was the first Christian in my family. Greg's words rattled me to the core of my being. They were words I needed to hear and yet words I didn't want to hear.

Why? Opposition awaited. And yet, this crisis of faith as a baby in the Lord served as a crucible in which I would grow, trust the Lord, and share my faith in the face of opposition.

It took eighteen months for me to come out. One by one I shared my new-found faith with my entire family. My maternal grandmother said scornfully, "Larry, how can you do this? No one in our family has ever believed in Jesus before." I've already mentioned how my father plainly stated, "That's fine. Just never share your faith with your grandmother (his mother)."

Many years have passed and much witnessing for the Lord has taken place. And yet, at times I still feel reluctant to share my faith. Such reluctance is a constant reality for the believer, especially if we're living out loud.

"...there is nothing new under the sun" (Ecclesiastes 1:9). Two-thousand years ago, the Apostle Paul wrote about the clash as he was on mission for God:

"For indeed, when we came to Macedonia, our bodies had no rest, but we were troubled on every side. *Outside were conflicts, inside were fears*" (2 Corinthians 7:5 italics mine).

What was true for Paul, and is true in my life, is true in yours also. But this question remains for all: Will we overcome the opposition or will we be overcome by the opposition?

In simple terms, overcoming opposition is to witness despite its presence. To be overcome by opposition is allowing it to silence our witness for Jesus.

In Acts 4 we see a very practical example of overcoming faith that inspires and instructs.

The scene: After healing a lame man in Jesus' name, Peter and John are arrested by the Jewish religious authorities, commanding them "not to speak at all nor teach in the name of Jesus" (Acts 4:18).

The response of Peter and John is telling:

"Whether it is right in the sight of God to listen to you more than to God, you judge. For we cannot but speak the things which we have seen and heard" (Acts 4:19-20).

The Great Commission had a greater influence upon their witness than the mandate of men. Underlying their boldness and courage was this principle for overcoming opposition: The salvation of people was more important than their personal safety.

After threatening them further, the religious authorities released Peter and John, who immediately went and reported to the other disciples "all that the chief priests and elders had said to them" (Acts 4:23).

During His earthly ministry, Jesus clearly stated "He who is not for Me is against Me" (Matthew 12:30, Luke 11:23). He would elaborate on the manifestation of the opposition to His witnesses elsewhere in the gospels (see also Matthew 5:11-12, Luke 21:12, John 15:20, John 16:1-2). In light of the Lord's instruction, the disciples would have expected push back.

Upon reporting about the great work of God amidst the great opposition of man, Peter, John, and the other disciples prayed, lifting their voices to God in one accord (Acts 4:23-30). Part of this prayer acknowledges opposition to God's plans and purposes, as they quote from Psalm 2:1-2:

Why did the nations rage,
And the people plot vain things?
The kings of the earth took their stand,
And the rulers were gathered together
against the LORD and against His Anointed One [Messiah]
(Acts 4:25-26).

It's evident from their prayer that the disciples understood opposition to God's plans and purposes not only from Jesus' teaching, but from the Bible itself, which at that time was strictly the Old Testament.

As they acknowledge the present opposition to their testimony, they cry out for boldness and courage:

"For truly against Your holy Servant Jesus, whom You anointed, both Herod and Pontius Pilate, with the Gentiles and the people of Israel, were gathered together to do whatever Your hand and Your purpose determined before to be done. Now, Lord, look on their threats, and grant to Your servants that with all boldness they may speak Your word" (Acts 4:27-29).

God answered their prayer immediately and powerfully:

And when they had prayed, the place where they were assembled together was shaken; and they were all filled with the Holy Spirit, and they spoke the word of God with boldness (Acts 4:31).

Prayer is essential for overcoming opposition to our witness.

Without Jesus we can do nothing (John 15:5), but through Christ and in His power, we can do all things (Philippians 4:13), including witnessing in the midst of opposition.

Overcoming opposition in our witness includes utterly depending on the Lord in prayer. Yes, the fear is real. Rejection is a possibility. Opposition is a certainty, and growing in America. But remember, their salvation is more important than our safety. And in the midst of it all, you and I have all the resources we need to accomplish all God calls us to do. His grace is sufficient, and God is faithful.

Alliance, Defiance, Or Silence

Francis Bellamy (1855-1931) was a Baptist minister's son from upstate New York. He distinguished himself in oratory at the University of Rochester before following his father to the pulpit, preaching at churches in New York and Boston. "Later in his life, while working for a family magazine called the *Youth's Companion*, he set to work on a patriotic program for schools around the country, commemorating Christopher Columbus' 400th anniversary of arriving in the New World.

Included in that program was the now famous "The Pledge of Allegiance," which Bellamy wrote in August 1892." [20]

> In its original form it read: "I pledge allegiance to my Flag and the Republic for which it stands, one nation, indivisible, with liberty and justice for all." In 1923, the words, "the Flag of the United States of America" were added. In 1954, in response to the Communist threat of those times, President Eisenhower encouraged Congress to add the words "under God," creating the 31-word pledge we say today. Today it reads: "I pledge allegiance to the flag of the United States of America, and to the republic for which it stands, one nation under God, indivisible, with liberty and justice for all." [21]

Today, the "under God" part is creating quite a stir in America. Yes, allegiance to His authority is polarizing.

In fact, allegiance to His authority has always been a polarizing proposition and at the center of the clash. We all have a choice—choose this day whom you will serve, God or man? (Joshua 24:15)

Jesus was not only the most polarizing figure in His day, He is the most polarizing person in history. And hence, those who declare allegiance to Him are now squared off against those who not only reject Him, but defy His authority.

Perhaps that's why Jesus' words resonate with us: "He who is not with Me is against Me" (Matthew 12:30, Luke 11:23).

The Apostle Paul is a prime example of one caught up in the storm of alliance or defiance to the authority of Jesus.

In Acts 9, after Saul (Paul) was converted he began preaching the gospel to the amazement of many:

> Immediately he preached the Christ in the synagogues, that He is the Son of God.
>
> Then all who heard were amazed, and said, "Is this not he who destroyed those who called on this name in Jerusalem, and has come here for that purpose, so that he might bring them bound to the chief priests?" But Saul increased all the more in strength, and confounded the Jews who dwelt in Damascus, proving that this Jesus is the Messiah [Christ] (Acts 9:20-22).

Saul, who acted in defiance of all things related to Jesus, was now allied with the Lord. And as passionately as he fought against the gospel, he now fought for the gospel. Defiance turned to alliance—this is the very power of God.

Those not willing to pledge allegiance to the Lord not only defy the gospel through unbelief, they also, at times, may actively try to silence it, as seen in the intense opposition to Saul.

> Now after many days were past, the Jews plotted to kill him. But their plot became known to Saul. And they watched the gates day and night, to kill him. Then the disciples took him by night and let him down through the wall in a large basket (Acts 9:23-25).

At this point in the narrative there is uncertainty and confusion among some of the disciples. I imagine their thinking was something along these lines: "What's the deal with Saul? We thought he was against us. Now he appears to be for us."

Saul was the real deal. It was no ruse. No trap. He was a bold believer, a believer who would not remain silent despite the threats of those who wanted to silence him:

> And when Saul had come to Jerusalem, he tried to join the disciples; but they were all afraid of him, and did not believe that he was a disciple. But Barnabas took him and brought him to the apostles. And he declared to them how he had seen the Lord on the road, and that He had spoken to him, and how he had preached boldly at Damascus in the name of Jesus. So he was with them at Jerusalem, coming in and going out. *And he spoke boldly in the name of the Lord Jesus and disputed against the Hellenists, but they attempted to kill him.* When the brethren found out, they brought him down to Caesarea and sent him out to Tarsus. (Acts 9:26-30) [*author emphasis*]

Paul lived out loud. His alliance to the Lord Jesus required it. Those in defiance of the Lord Jesus sought to silence the propagation of the gospel.

Fast forward to our present cultural environment.

Here in the United States of America, hostility to Christianity and the gospel is rising at an alarming pace. And yet, as we see, there is nothing new under the sun.

For those of us who pledge allegiance to Jesus, the question is this: Will we stay silent about our faith, or will we "live out loud," like the Apostle Paul? Will we engage those in defiance of the gospel who seek to silence our witness? We all have a choice.

What kind of threats do you face today to keep silent about Jesus and to keep your faith in the closet? Have you brought them before the Lord of Glory, who desires we live out loud, glorifying His name? He knows the pressure. He knows the threats. He knows the challenges you and I face this moment. And He's ready to meet us at our point of need.

Practically speaking, to live out loud is to express our alliance to Christ. And in this way our alliance to Christ is defiance against silence.

Therefore, LORD, give us the grace and faith to live out loud, proclaiming Your gospel among an increasingly hostile world that so desperately needs You. Amen.

Sing to the LORD, bless His name;
Proclaim the good news of His salvation from day to day.

Declare His glory among the nations,
His wonders among all peoples (Psalm 96:2-3).

Overcome Or Be Overcome

Just as opposing air masses bring severe springtime weather when they collide, the spiritual clash between light and darkness will often be severe as well.

And as the tempest of opposition roared against our Christian brothers and sisters in the early church, the same whirlwind of opposition blows against our Christian testimony today.

The issue for us in the midst of our present environment of increasing pushback against the faith is this: We will either overcome our opposition or be overcome by it.

To be overcome is to succumb to the goal of persecution that opposition brings, which as we mentioned earlier is to silence our voice and eliminate our influence.

To overcome means we continue to walk in the light of the Lord—following Him. This is to follow the truth regardless of the consequences. To overcome also means to trust in the Lord through the power of prayer—asking for the boldness and courage to live out loud.

May the Lord, by His grace, grant us all we need to do just that. Amen.

"For whatever is born of God overcomes the world. And this is the victory that has overcome the world—our faith" (1 John 5:4)

Chapter 4

Friends Not Foes

Wind is an enemy of the tennis player, right? Well, not so fast. It's true that wind can wreak havoc on the path of the furry yellow ball as it passes from one side of the tennis court to the other. Any tennis player could tell you that, including me.

I began playing competitive tennis in Florida when I was ten years old, barnstormed the state during my teenage years while competing on the junior circuit, and played tennis throughout college. After my playing career ended, I coached tennis professionally for fourteen years—in Florida at tennis clubs and academies for five years and as an assistant tennis coach at East Tennessee State University for nine years.

As you might imagine, I've played and coached in various conditions, including strong and gusty winds. And sometimes blustery conditions are downright nasty. At the least they are challenging.

I've often coached up my players on a windy day, because windy conditions need not be an enemy. They may be a friend. If you cope with the wind better than your opponent, a gale may work for you rather than against you.

There is a physical side to coping with the wind. With a strong tailwind (at your back), more topspin is important, while hitting the ball much flatter is preferable against a sharp breeze. With crazy crosswinds, the general play is to keep the ball more in the center of the court. If you play tennis you understand. If not, all you need to know is there is a proper strategy—hit the ball in such a way as to allow the wind to work for you, not against you.

In addition to the physical strategy, the mental approach is also critical. In fact, if one really wants a mental edge when facing windy conditions during a competitive tennis match, then it is better to believe that the wind is a friend, not a foe.

In America's current spiritual climate, we often face blustery conditions. As we seek to effectively serve the Lord and others in a rising gale of persecution, we must develop strategies and perceptions in line with God's Word.

Specifically, as we think of people—difficult people—hostile people—people who some might call enemies of the faith—we need to see them as God sees them; see them through the prism of His Word. And when we do, we'll be better equipped to share His love and proclaim the truth in love with people who need Jesus—even those we perceive as enemies.

In our study we come to a personal place: personal evangelism. Evangelism in our context includes prayer, demonstrating God's love in deed, and proclaiming God's truth in word.

Our starting point is learning to regard people as friends, not foes. And as we unpack this foundational concept, I hope we'll see people more as God sees them, have our hearts more broken for the lost, and be more compelled to reach out to people who need the Lord.

The Culture, The People And The True Enemy

As we introduced our study we defined the culture as "a way of life for a group of people—the behaviors, beliefs, values, and symbols they accept, generally, without thinking about them, and that are passed along by communication and imitation from one generation to the next."

Simply, a culture is how and why people do things. We can clearly place people at the center of culture, because in one sense people *are* the culture and are the movers and shakers of cultural shift, which at that moment is trending away from God.

We've noted that since our culture is moving away from our Judeo-Christian moorings, it's becoming increasingly hostile to the church and our Christian faith.

As we live for Christ, walk in the light, and proclaim the gospel, we are going to create a reaction and a response that's powerful. The Apostle Paul wrote: "For the message of the cross is foolishness to those who are perishing, but to us who are being saved it is the power of God" (1 Corinthians 1:18).

And yet, those who are perishing—who are rejecting us and our message—are the very ones God is also calling us to love, serve and pray for, and witness to. And we'll see this going forward.

People are not our enemy. Satan and his minions are, as we've touched upon already. 1 Peter 5:8 states, "Be sober, be vigilant; because your adversary the devil walks about like a roaring lion, seeking whom he may devour." The Apostle Paul added: "For we do not wrestle against flesh and blood, but against principalities, against the rulers of the darkness of this age, against spiritual hosts of wickedness in the heavenly places" (Ephesians 6:12). The enemy of our souls would do anything and everything within his power to keep us from sharing the life-giving message of the gospel.

He hates God's children to the core, and his desire is to thwart any and every attempt to share the gospel with anyone at any time. Not only does he want to defeat us, he would destroy us if he could.

The devil's strategy of opposing our Christian life is referred to by the Apostle Paul in Ephesians 6:11 as "wiles of the devil."

If it weren't enough that the devil opposes our evangelistic efforts at every turn, he also exerts great effort in opposing the hearing, understanding, and reception of the gospel message among people who've not yet met Christ. In short, he not only opposes we who seek to share, but also those who need to hear the gospel: "But even if our gospel is veiled, it is veiled to those who are perishing, whose minds the god of this age has blinded, who do not believe, lest the light of the gospel of the glory of Christ, who is the image of God, should shine on them" (2 Corinthians 4:3-4)

The people we seek to reach are in spiritual bondage and our task is to proclaim the message of liberation and freedom found in the person of Jesus Christ. As we think about reaching people, let's distinguish between the culture, people, and our true enemy.

Love Your Neighbor...And Your Enemy.

Interestingly, it is in the context of relationships where personal evangelism takes place. Yes, we're in a battle, but our battle is not with flesh and blood. Rather, it's spiritual in nature. Jesus said some interesting things about human adversaries, even human "enemies."

Jesus, a friend of sinners, told His followers to love all people, including their enemies, the same way He did. This is the nature of relationships in God's Kingdom. The Lord elaborates:

> "You have heard that it was said, "You shall love your neighbor and hate your enemy." But I say to you, love your enemies, bless those who curse you, do good to those who hate you, and pray for those who spitefully use you and persecute you, that you may be sons of your Father in heaven; for He makes His sun rise on the evil and on the good, and sends rain on the just and on the unjust. For if you love those who love you, what reward have you? Do not even the tax collectors do the same? And if you greet your brethren only, what do you do more than others? Do not even the tax collectors do so? Therefore you shall be perfect, just as your Father in heaven is perfect" (Matthew 5:43-48).

When Jesus was asked in Matthew 23:36 what the greatest commandment was, He responded, "'You shall love the LORD your God with all your heart, with all your soul, and with all your mind.' This is the first and greatest commandment. And the second is like it: 'You shall love your neighbor as yourself.'" On these two commandments hang all the Law and the Prophets" (Matthew 22:37-40).

What do we make of Jesus' commandment to "love your neighbor as yourself"?

In one sense it speaks of relationship. We can't love someone we don't know. The phrase: "You shall love your neighbor as yourself" is a direct quote from Leviticus 19:18. In fact, it is the most quoted Old Testament text in the entire New Testament (see also Matthew 5:43, 19:19; Mark 12:31, 33; Luke 10:27; Romans 13:9; Galatians 5:14;

James 2:8). When God repeats Himself, you can be sure it's very important. Jesus, in declaring the greatest commandments, communicates the centrality of relationships—relationship with God and relationship with others.

The Counter Culture Of Personal Relationships

Relationships and personal evangelism go hand in hand. Personal evangelism is personal—pun intended. Relationships that are intentional are the platform on which the process occurs.

In our twenty-first century techno-dominated culture, people speed date, Snapchat, Instagram one another, text and relate and communicate via a myriad of other technologies. But what of it? Research into human behavior shows our technology inhibits rather than enhances our personal connectedness to one another. Face to face and eye to eye is still the gold-standard for personal communication.

In his book *Eats with Sinners*, Arron Chambers writes:

> Relationships are the key to reaching lost people. I define evangelism as "an intentional relationship through which someone is introduced to Jesus Christ." Healthy relationships are essential if we want to have the kind of life God intended for all of us, and they are also essential if we want to reach lost people like Jesus did.[22]

A survey conducted by Church Growth, Inc. revealed what should be obvious: most people come to a saving faith in Jesus through an intentional relationship. They asked more than 10,000 people, "What was most responsible for your coming to Christ and this church?" Seventy-nine percent responded, "A friend or relative invited me."[23]

As His servants, we are called to follow our King, developing relationships with people who've not yet met Jesus, and to be salt and light to the world.

Beautiful And Broken

The wonder of a newborn baby is awe-inspiring. The miracle of new life reminds us of God's blessing bestowed upon the human race: "So God created man in His own image; in the image of God He created him; male and female He created them" (Genesis 1:27).

Beautiful is that precious human being coming into the world. And we take delight in the new arrival. Though we may be tempted to gaze upon the infant and think "perfect," we know better.

There will come a time in the not-so-distant future when that baby grows into a little child, able to express an aspect of our identity as human beings that is both undeniable and undesirable. We are not perfect—we are broken. The curse of sin mars our role as image-bearers of the Creator God.

Beautiful yes. Yet, broken at the same time. This paradox of our identity as human beings, beautiful yet broken, has led philosophers, theologians and others throughout history to attempt reconcile this paradox—this identity crisis—if you will.

Who am I? Who are you? And why does it matter? These are the kinds of questions reverberating through our culture, where the tempest of opposition to our faith continues to increase.

How then do we engage a culture seeking to dislodge itself from the tether called morality—that morality being transcendent, absolute, and God-given?

Thoughtfully and compassionately.

May I suggest we become conversant in the dominant current cultural issues. For example, it would do us well to have a working understanding of things like Millennials, gender issues, race relations, the rise of the nones—those who have no religious affiliation—and the effect of post-modernism on our society. Learning from Christian commentators engaging these and other issues of the day is certainly a benefit and will enhance our witness.

Let's briefly touch upon one of these—gender issues. The hot-button topic of gender today is simply one manifestation of a broader issue humankind has faced for millennia—identity. We see Jesus providing a compassionate example to people struggling with identity issues. He gently addressed the woman caught in adultery (John 8:1-11), forgave a prostitute (Luke 7:36-50), and ministered to a societal misfit (the Samaritan woman) in John 4:4-42.

And while some may express righteous indignation toward those who seek to legitimize gender confusion, let's not forget those precious, broken people who struggle to find their identity.

Jesus compassionately comes to seek and to save those who are lost, even those wallowing in the brokenness of gender confusion. Regardless of how people struggle with identity, all of us share in the brokenness of sin, which is also an identity issue.

Our shared brokenness, namely our fractured relationship with God, is ultimately mended in the person of Jesus and in His glorious gospel. And guess what? You and I have been given the ministry of reconciliation as His ambassadors:

> "Now all things are of God, who has reconciled us to Himself through Jesus Christ, and has given us the ministry of reconciliation, that is, that God was in Christ reconciling the world to Himself, not imputing their trespasses to them, and has committed to us the word of reconciliation" (2 Corinthians 5:18-19).

May we never forget the inestimable value people are to God, even those we're tempted to deem our enemies. He is the healer of the broken-hearted and the restorer of that which is broken. In the gospel, the Lord desires all who are broken by sin to be made beautiful through the righteousness of Christ. God's desire and design for humanity is that people find their ultimate identity, not in who we are, but in *Whose* we are.

No Lost Causes

Have you ever felt tempted to quit praying for a lost person in your sphere of influence—be it a family member, long-time friend, or anyone else you've known for a period of years? It's one thing to talk about persevering in prayer. It's another thing to do it.

Why?

Because somewhere within may lurk the idea that there is no way this person is going to come to faith. The thinking may includes sentiments like:

"If you only knew them. They're reprobate."

"They're never going to change."

"They don't want to hear about Jesus. In fact, they're downright hostile to the gospel."

"I hate to say this, but they are a lost cause."

Have you been there? Have you harbored such thoughts? It pains me to say this, but I have.

I have a biblical and not so subtle response to this kind of thinking: not so fast.

We have a famous example of one who, if it were possible, certainly would have qualified as a "lost cause." Yet, with God all things are possible, including the salvation of the most unlikely of people.

Let me introduce—drumroll please—Saul of Tarsus.

We first meet Saul in the New Testament book of Acts. A righteous man, Stephen, a man full of faith and of the Holy Spirit (Acts 6:5), and a man full of grace and power (Acts 6:8), gave a powerful testimony about Christ and was martyred for his faith (Acts 7). It is at Stephen's execution that we first meet Saul:

> ...and they cast him out of the city and stoned him. And the witnesses laid down their clothes at the feet of a young man named Saul. And they stoned Stephen as he was calling on God and saying, "Lord Jesus, receive my spirit. *Now Saul was consenting to his death.* At that time a great persecution arose against the church which was at Jerusalem; and they were all scattered throughout the regions of Judea and Samaria, except the apostles. *As for Saul, he made havoc of the church, entering every house, and dragging off men and women,*

committing them to prison (Acts 7:58-59, Acts 8:1, 3, italics mine).

We can only imagine the early believers response to Saul's raging persecution. It seems to me there were two camps of thinking regarding his rampage.

First, there may have been a group of believers who viewed Saul as a "madman," as "bad news," and someone to avoid at all times in all situations. Is it possible there were some followers of Jesus who may have coined Saul a "lost cause?" Here was this learned religious Jewish man who certainly would have, to some degree, been exposed to Jesus' teaching and would have known of His miracles and renown during His earthly ministry. And yet, he categorically rejected everyone and everything associated with Jesus.

On the other hand, there must have been those disciples who remembered Jesus' command to "love your enemies, bless those who curse you, do good to those who hate you, and pray for those who spitefully use you and persecute you" (Matthew 5:44).

Wow. This is not a natural response. Rather it's a *supernatural* response—and one I believe would have been undertaken by some of Jesus' faithful followers in response to Saul's opposition and persecution.

And you say, "How?"

Through an attitude of love and compassion for Saul's spiritual lostness along with prayer for his salvation.

Apart from Stephen's testimony, there is no biblical record of anyone witnessing to Saul. But in Acts 9:1-6, Jesus came to seek and to save this one who was lost, bringing Saul out of the Kingdom of Darkness and into the Kingdom of Light:

The Apostle Paul would later write: "Do not be overcome by evil, but overcome evil with good" (Romans 12:21).

You most likely don't know a "Saul-like" figure personally. But you definitely know people who are lost and difficult to love, serve, and pray for. You may even have someone you're tempted to coin a lost cause.

Well, not so fast.

Remember the Apostle Paul, and if you're so inclined, think about your own faith journey. I can tell you I only uttered the name of Jesus Christ in vain for the first twenty-three years of my life. Yes, I was an enemy of God. I'm eternally grateful that people witnessed to me, prayed for me, and showed me God's love. And I'm eternally grateful to God for saving me.

So, persevere in prayer, persevere in good works, persevere in love, and persevere in proclaiming the good news of Jesus. And remember, there are no lost causes, just lost people.

The Inclusivity Of The Gospel

Divisiveness is the one word that characterizes our present cultural condition. The politically-correct crowd gets offended seemingly at just about anything and many so-called leaders in our nation want to create polarization and conflict among people.

While our culture and many in it are crying out "separation," the gospel cries out "reconciliation"—"For God so loved the world that He gave His only begotten Son, that whoever believes in Him should not perish but have everlasting life" (John 3:16). The "whosoever" part is huge for us ministers of reconciliation to get straight. We need to understand the gospel is not about us and them. It's about "we"—as in we all as human beings have a problem called sin. And because we all are estranged from God because of our sin, we all need reconciliation with God through faith in Jesus, the "Prince of Peace" (Isaiah 9:6).

Today, there are divides in our culture that seek to pit us against one another. But guess what? The gospel is bigger and more powerful than any cultural divide that exists, real or otherwise. But as we turn back to the book of Acts, we revisit another "us vs. them" cultural divide that the gospel overcomes. It is the "Jewish-Gentile" divide—which we touched on earlier. That divide was a huge deal for the church to reconcile going forward.

When the church was born in Acts 2, the 3000 saved were Jews who were attending the Jewish feast of Shavuot, better known to us as

Pentecost. As we've mentioned earlier in our study, the church was initially considered just another Jewish sect. When God called Peter to preach the gospel to Cornelius and his household, they became the first Gentile converts to Jesus. Gentile inclusion in the Kingdom was always God's plan:

> Indeed He says, "It is too small a thing that You should be My Servant to raise up the tribes of Jacob, And to restore the preserved ones of Israel; *I will also give You as a light to the Gentiles, that You should be My salvation to the ends of the earth'"* (Isaiah 49:6; see also Isaiah 42:6, italics mine)

So when God calls Peter to proclaim the good news of Messiah Jesus to Cornelius, a Gentile, it's rather surprising that Peter initially resists the Lord, apparently forgetting the Old Testament promises concerning the inclusion of Gentiles in the Kingdom.

Though we've already covered this narrative, I want us to see another angle. There is much here to glean regarding gospel inclusiveness. After Peter and Cornelius compare notes regarding God's divine appointment (Acts 10:24-33), Peter says:

> "*In truth I perceive that God shows no partiality.* But in every nation whoever fears Him and works righteousness is accepted by Him. The word which God sent to the children of Israel, preaching peace through Jesus Christ—He is Lord of all" (Acts 10:34-36, italics mine).

Peter then went on to share the gospel, affirming the inclusiveness of the gospel message. Still, when Cornelius and his household are saved, Peter is amazed:

> "And He [Jesus] commanded us to preach to the people, and to testify that it is He who was ordained by God to be Judge of the living and the dead. To Him all the prophets witness that, through His name, whoever believes in Him will receive remission of sins." While Peter was still speaking these words, the Holy Spirit fell upon all those who heard the word. And

those of the circumcision who believed were astonished, as many as came with Peter, because the gift of the Holy Spirit had been poured out on the Gentiles also (Acts 10:42-45).

Following this remarkable series of events, the disciples have a meeting of the minds in Acts 11. This fulfillment of prophecy startled the apostles and other brethren, causing them to confront Peter (Acts 11:1-3). After Peter explains, his Jewish brethren glorify God:

> "If therefore God gave them the same gift as He gave us when we believed on the Lord Jesus Christ, who was I that I could withstand God?" When they heard these things they became silent; and they glorified God, saying, "Then God has also granted to the Gentiles repentance to life" (Acts 11:17-18).

As I like to say on occasion: "It's not about your "Jewishness" or your "Gentileness""—it's about your "Jesusness"—do you know Him? This was true in the first century and is true today.

One of the beautiful aspects of the church of Jesus is that He has called and is calling a people "out of every tribe and tongue and people and nation" (Revelation 5:9, 7:9).

Consequently the gospel transcends any divide a certain culture may devise.

Additionally, God is "not willing that anyone should perish but that all should come to repentance" (2 Peter 3:9).

May we rejoice in God's plan for mankind, praising Him and thanking Him for the inclusive nature of the gospel message.

The Testimony Of Love, Joy, And Peace

Have you thought of your personal relationship with the Lord as having an impact on your witness? I would imagine in terms of what you say or don't say or do or don't do—yes. But what about in terms of simply "being"? By that I'm referring to our unspoken and undemonstrated witness.

Our testimony has the potential to be radiant in beauty as we reflect the Lord through the manifestation of the fruit of the Spirit.

"But the fruit of the Spirit is love, joy, peace, long-suffering, kindness, goodness, faithfulness, gentleness and self-control" (Galatians 5:22).

Now people may quibble with our words, but there is no denying the power of a joyful countenance on the servant who loves Jesus. I don't know what else to call it except the "Jesus look." You may have your own expression.

The "Jesus look" is what someone sees in a faithful believer, one who exudes the "joy of the Lord." That joy can only be produced by Him, not our circumstances. This is the fruit of the Spirit described in Galatians 5.

Case in point: Many years ago while I was a tennis coach in East Tennessee, we had a gentleman named Mike who regularly played in our tennis tournaments. On other occasions, I'd see Mike at the tennis courts where I gave private lessons. Mike always had a smile on his face and his joy was contagious. It was a powerful testimony and one that caused me to take notice.

One day I was teaching a tennis lesson and Mike was playing on an adjacent court. This was the day I was going to confront him. I had to know. If my theory about Mike being a believer was wrong, then I would have to throw the whole "joy of the Lord" theory out the proverbial window.

I walked to him and said, "Mike, I want to ask you something."

He strolled over with that same joyful expression on his face. "Yes?"

I just blurted it out. "You love Jesus, don't you?" He grinned even more. "Yes. Yes I do."

"Good. I thought you did because you exude the joy of the Lord." How's that for a blunt, direct confrontation?

The fruit of the Spirit can be quite powerful in our witness to others. Whether we realize it or not people are always watching.

The book of 2 Corinthians tells us that we are living epistles. An epistle is a letter, and as such, it is read. Paul wrote to the believers at Corinth:

"You are our epistle written in our hearts, known and read by all men; clearly you are an epistle of Christ, ministered by us, written not with ink, but by the Spirit of the living God, not on tablets of stone but on tablets of flesh, that is, of the heart" (2 Corinthians 3:2-3).

The implication is that people are always watching and reading us. Not only our words and deeds are in play, but also our countenance.

I'm a big fan of the movie, *Monsters Inc.* I still like watching it with our children, Elijah and Shoshanna, even though they're teenagers today. One of my favorite characters is Roz. In this animated comedy, Roz is the ever watching and listening secretary who keeps things in the Scare Factory in order. There are a few scenes in the movie where she reminds one of the factory workers, named Mike Wazowski, played by Billy Crystal, that she's watching. In fact, she reminds him on more than one occasion. "Wazowski, I'm watching you. Always watching."

Whether we realize it or not, people are watching you and me. Always watching.

At the University of Florida in the mid-1980s, before my salvation experience, I ran into Matt on campus. He grew up in my neighborhood. I remembered two things about Matt: he was an awesome drummer and he got into lots of trouble. I hadn't seen him in a few years, but the moment I saw him I could tell something was different, very different.

He had a peaceful countenance, and the tone of his words was also filled with peace. Matt shared with me that he'd become a Christian. He said he was recording a Christian concert at a local TV station and wondered if I wanted to hang out.

I said, "No thanks," and went on my way. In all honesty, his peaceful countenance freaked me out. It scared me, because it was powerful and unique. I didn't understand it. And, at the time, I didn't want to understand it.

While we should aspire to know Christ intimately and experience and express the fruit of the Spirit in abundance, the response of others to that expression will be mixed. People may be attracted to or repelled by it. The countenance of God's glory in a person may evoke fear. That was certainly the case after Moses had spent forty days with the Lord on Mount Sinai. Upon coming down, the Israelites were afraid to come near Moses because his appearance had changed (Exodus 34:29-30).

Remember that the love, joy, and peace we express is a powerful testimony to those who are watching. May each of us be a living epistle that's a compelling read to the Rozs and others in our life. Because they're watching...always watching.

Let us embrace the Kingdom reality that people, even our human "enemies," are not foes to fight with, avoid or conquer, but friends who need to be loved with the love of God and won over for the Lord.

Navigating differences with others amidst the cultural divide takes wisdom and discernment, but most importantly it takes love. We are called to "...not be overcome by evil, but overcome evil with good" (Romans 12:21). May we, by the grace of God, do just that.

Chapter 5

A Surprising Catalyst

By most measures, the Chicago Fire of 1871 was a catastrophe that left only devastation. "At the time, the Windy City's population was 330,000, making it the fourth largest city in America.

Incredibly, from the time the inferno began on Sunday evening October 8 to the time flames subsided Tuesday morning, October 11–The Great Fire had consumed more than three square miles (some 2,000 acres) of the city, taken 300 lives, left 100,000 without shelter (about a third of the population), destroyed 18,000 buildings, and damaged property valued at nearly $200 million." [24]

> "During the week immediately leading up to the blaze, not a single drop of rain fell at all. To make matters worse, the humidity plunged below thirty percent as winds increased out of the southwest at over twenty mph on the evening the first flames were spotted.
>
> The combination of the dry, windy weather and a city infrastructure constructed almost entirely of wood caused the flames to spread quickly. Carried by the wind, embers ignited building after building, allowing the fire to become out of control quickly." [25]

Interestingly, the aftermath of the Great Fire didn't bring self-pity, quit, or resignation among Chicagoans. Rather, what inspired them was what had transpired amidst their challenging circumstance. Following the Great Fire began a period known as the Great Rebuilding. A great many buildings were rebuilt to duplicate the pre-fire construction; many lasting over 70 years. It was, in fact, a tragedy that served as the catalyst for triumph, especially in architecture.

> "The architects who rebuilt Chicago comprised one of the greatest concentrations of creative architectural talent in U. S. history. From their ideas and work emerged the Chicago School, which is synonymous with the development and mastery of steel framing and the consequent development of tall buildings as the dominant feature of the urban skyline.
>
> In fact, these architectural pioneers in Chicago during the Great Rebuilding made it both technically and commercially viable to build a new class of taller buildings. By 1888, these tall buildings were being labelled "skyscrapers." Chicago initially led the way in skyscraper design, with many constructed in the center of the financial district during the late 1880s and early 1890s." [26]

The paradox of the Chicago Fire was that a tragedy turned into triumph. And one could ask: "How could a devastating fire be so positively catalytic, transforming an entire city? How does something so negative serve as a powerful force for good?"

The Christian life is full of paradoxes, seemingly absurd propositions that when investigated prove to be true. There are theological paradoxes. For example, we believe in the Trinity, that God is one and God is three. One God eternally exists as three distinct Persons—Father, Son, and Spirit. The oneness of God is the plurality of Persons in community. We also have living paradoxes—like slavery leads to freedom (Romans 6:18, 1 Corinthians 7:22) and the foolish are wise (1 Corinthians 3:18, 4:10).

As we think about the Great Commission, we engage another paradox—the power of persecution. On a human level, we may initially perceive persecution as being undesirable, counterproductive, or simply bad. Yet, upon further inspection, through the eyes of faith, we will see persecution as something else—something powerful. In simple terms, persecution can be catalytic, not catastrophic.

As we look at today's cultural landscape, we see many people fanning the flame of opposition against the Christian faith. Conditions appear to be worsening. The growing gale of persecution in America appears to be causing a firestorm burning out of control. But is this really the case?

> And we know that all things [including persecution] work together for good to those who love God, to those who are the called according to His purpose (Romans 8:28).

What people may do or say to inhibit the expression of our Christian faith, can be a tool for good in the Hand of God, whose plans and purposes will not and cannot be thwarted. Rest assured, nothing takes our great God by surprise. He is the Alpha and Omega, knowing the end from the beginning.

As we continue learning lessons from the book of Acts, I want to briefly highlight three ways the Lord used persecution to accomplish His plans and purposes in the early church and apply those ways to our present walk with the Lord.

Persecution accomplished three things in the early church:

It was catalytic.

It confirmed Jesus' words.

It made unity imperative.

Persecution Was Catalytic

> Remember Jesus' words to the disciples just before His ascension:

> "But you shall receive power when the Holy Spirit has come upon you; and you shall be witnesses to Me in Jerusalem, and in all Judea and Samaria, and to the end of the earth" (Acts 1:8).

It was persecution that propelled the disciples to share the gospel "to the end of the earth." And we see the genesis of this dynamic in Acts 8:1-5:

Now Saul was consenting to his death. *At that time a great persecution arose against the church which was at Jerusalem; and they were all scattered throughout the regions of Judea and Samaria,* except the apostles. And devout men carried Stephen to his burial, and made great lamentation over him. As for Saul, he made havoc of the church, entering every house, and dragging off men and women, committing them to prison. *Therefore those who were scattered went everywhere preaching the word.* Then Philip went down to the city of Samaria and preached Christ to them (italics mine).

Persecution was both a crucible and catalyst in the early church—and the result of this scattering was just the opposite of the desire and design of the persecutors.

Now those who were scattered after the persecution that arose over Stephen traveled as far as Phoenicia, Cyprus, and Antioch, preaching the word to no one but the Jews only. But some of them were men from Cyprus and Cyrene, who, when they had come to Antioch, spoke to the Hellenists, preaching the Lord Jesus. And the hand of the Lord was with them, *and a great number believed and turned to the Lord* (Acts 11:19-21, italics mine).

This is the church's wake-up call of opportunity for action.

In response to the gale of growing persecution, will we allow the Lord to use persecution in a catalytic fashion to mobilize us, or will we allow it to paralyze our Christian testimony?

In one sense, our historical bubble of blessing, devoid of much persecution compared with the rest of the world, has burst. And it seems to me this new season of increased opposition to our faith may also be catalytic in awaking us out of spiritual apathy or lethargy.

The Apostle Paul wrote: "And do this, knowing the time, *that now it is high time to awake out of sleep;* for now our salvation is nearer than when we first believed" (Romans 13:11, italics mine).

Just as there was a "now" for the church in Rome, the original recipients of this message, there is a "now" moment for the American church—a moment of decision—a decision to become more involved in the things of God and more committed to the Great Commission.

Will we allow the gale of persecution to blow us off course—to paralyze us—or will we see it as a springboard, by God's grace—as a means of mobilizing us.

We can live out loud or be silent. We can shirk back from the challenge or lean into it. We can allow the gale of persecution to create fear leading to inaction or we can view it as an opportunity for increased faith in the Lord that allows the wind of the Spirit to move us to action.

As we walk by faith in the power of the Holy Spirit, we can trust He will use challenges to our faith as opportunities, not obstacles—in order to fulfill His plans and purposes in this season of life in the American experiment.

So, my brother and sisters, let us walk by faith, not fear, into the gale.

Persecution Confirmed Jesus' Words

The disciples were carried along by the power of the Holy Spirit as they were scattered and spread the gospel, as Jesus had foretold. As they experienced the explosion of church growth amidst the intense opposition and persecution, I wonder how often they would have reminded themselves of Jesus' words, when He stated, "I will build My church, and the gates of Hades shall not prevail against it" (Matthew 16:18).

Jesus spoke of persecution throughout His earthly ministry. We note two bookends of teaching on the topic, first with words from His first sermon, the Sermon on the Mount:

> "Blessed are those who are persecuted for righteousness' sake, For theirs is the kingdom of heaven. Blessed are you when they revile and persecute you, and say all kinds of evil against you falsely for My sake" (Matthew 5:10-11).

And near the end of His earthly ministry in the upper room, just before Jesus is taken, He leaves the disciples with this promise:

> Remember the word that I said to you, "A servant is not greater than his master. If they persecuted Me, they will also persecute you" (John 15:20).

In Acts 5, the Lord was moving mightily through the Apostles and the church grew tremendously:

> Through the hands of the apostles many signs and wonders were done among the people. And believers were increasingly added to the Lord, multitudes of both men and women. Also a multitude gathered from the surrounding cities to Jerusalem, bringing sick people and those who were tormented by unclean spirits, and they were all healed (Acts 5:12, 14, 16).

In response, the High Priest and Sadducees looked upon this ministry with jealousy and rage, imprisoning the Apostles (Acts 5:18). Upon being released by an angel, the Apostles, undeterred, go right back to preaching the gospel at the Temple (Acts 5:20). And again, they're taken, this time to testify before the Council. Upon defying the Jewish religious leadership's demand to not teach in Jesus' name, Peter and the apostles plainly powerfully state in Acts 5:29: *"We must obey God rather than men."*

Although the Council wanted to put them to death, Gamaliel, the most prominent rabbi of the time and the Apostle Paul's teacher prior to his conversion, urged the Council to release them, reasoning: If their movement is not from God, it will fade as with previous messianic "pretenders" (Acts 5:33-38). But then he added, "but if it is of God, you cannot overthrow it—lest you even be found to fight against God" (Acts 5:39). The Council took Gamaliel's advice, but not before flogging the Apostles and again commanding them to refrain from speaking in Jesus' name.

The Apostle's response should inspire our witness amidst our own gale warnings: "So they departed from the presence of the council, rejoicing that they were counted worthy to suffer shame for His name" (Acts 5:41).

Their rejoicing was a result of their blessing. Is there any doubt they would have had these words of Jesus' in their heart as they identified with Him through their suffering: "Blessed are those who are persecuted for righteousness' sake…Rejoice and be exceedingly glad, for great is your reward in heaven, for so they persecuted the prophets who were before you" (Matthew 5:10, 12).

Persecution confirmed the words of Christ, but also deepened the communion of those who would suffer for His name's sake, as Paul noted in Philippians 3:10: "…that I may know Him and the power of His resurrection, and the fellowship of His sufferings, being conformed to His death" (Philippians 3:10).

For now, remember that the blessing of rejection as a follower of Jesus is a unique aspect of our walk with Him. On a human level, rejection is difficult, uncomfortable and at times downright painful. Yet, in the spiritual, it is a critical component in fully developing our relationship with Christ. To God be the Glory!

Following the Lord is a path marked with suffering, yet at the same time, a pathway to blessing—another paradox. His words would no doubt have affirmed the disciple's experience.

Persecution Made Unity Imperative

After hearing of the phenomenal growth of the church, Barnabas went to Antioch to encourage the believers:

> The news about them reached the ears of the church at Jerusalem, and they sent Barnabas off to Antioch. Then when he arrived and witnessed the grace of God, *he rejoiced and began to encourage them all with resolute heart to remain true to the Lord* (Acts 11:22-23, italics mine).

Why did Barnabas encourage them to remain true to the Lord? Because the fiery darts of persecution sought to scatter and silence them, for a house divided cannot stand. Unity in the Lord was paramount in continuing to fight the good fight of faith amidst the opposition and persecution. To remain true to the Lord is to remain committed to each other.

As the Apostle Paul exhorted the church in Ephesus:

> I, therefore, the prisoner of the Lord, beseech you to walk worthy of the calling with which you were called, with all lowliness and gentleness, with long-suffering, bearing with one another in love, endeavoring to keep the unity of the Spirit in the bond of peace. There is one body and one Spirit, just as you were called in one hope of your calling; one Lord, one faith, one baptism; one God and Father of all, who is above all, and through all, and in you all (Ephesians 4:1-6)

In his work called *Apology*, the Latin apologist Tertullian made this now-famous comment: "The oftener we are mown down by you, the more in number we grow; the blood of Christians is seed." [27] Somehow, the suffering of some Christians spurred others to more faithful living. The apostle Paul noted that "most of the brethren, trusting in the Lord because of my imprisonment, have far more courage to speak the Word of God without fear" (Philippians 1:14). Through all the terrible persecutions of the early centuries the church continued to grow.

Jesus knew the importance of unity among the saints. He said in Matthew 12:25, "Every kingdom divided against itself is brought to desolation, and every city or house divided against itself will not stand." Later the Lord prayed for the house of God, the church, "that they all may be one, as You, Father, are in Me, and I in You; that they also may be one in Us, that the world may believe that You sent Me" (John 17:21).

Biblical unity is key, as we earlier spent an entire chapter unpacking the concept. Majoring on the majors is critical. And loving one another is essential. Our ministry must begin with the household of faith, then fanning out, reaching out to people together.

Parting Shots On Persecution

Through much of our history, the church in America has

experienced a relative lack of persecution when compared to much of our brethren around the world. Today, this is changing before our very eyes, as open hostility, opposition and persecution to believers in America grows at increasing speed.

How shall we then live considering this growing persecution? Our first century brothers and sisters have informed, instructed, and inspired us.

First, we should see persecution not as catastrophic, but catalytic for our witness. Not an obstacle, but an opportunity. As persecution galvanized the early church, we should be galvanized to keep the main thing the main thing—and what is that main thing? It is this: With a resolute heart, remain true to the Lord. Dietrich Bonhoeffer said in the midst of World War II, "May God in His mercy lead us through these times; but above all, may He lead us to Himself." [28] As we abide in Christ, He will empower and work though our witness, even in the face of increasing persecution, as we have seen in the book of Acts.

Next, remember the words of the Lord. Persecution is an affirmation that God's Word is true. And on a personal basis, persecution can serve as a confirmation that we are living out loud, as the Lord Jesus commanded us to do and as those first century believers did.

Finally, persecution should serve to crystalize our unity of purpose as God's people—to know Him and make Him known. We see that purpose exemplified as we track with the early church in the book of Acts. So encourage one another, exhort one another, pray for one another, and stand with one another in the Great Commission, walking together hand in hand into the gale.

Chapter 6

Navigating Cultural Waters

Exhilarating. This was how the blend of wind, speed, and sailing on a beautiful Saturday summer afternoon upon a Tennessee lake made me feel. I was having a blast with two buddies from church. One of my friends, Dave, who owned the sailboat, allowed me to take the helm and captain the ship—okay, it was just a twenty footer.

The wind was blowing strong, but not too strong. And with the perfect combination of wind, sail settings, and the mark to which I steered the sailboat, we moved fast.

During one brief sequence of time, Dave was thrilled and said he thought this was the fastest his boat had traveled on water. I was blown away, because it was the first time in many years that I'd been on a sailboat, much less taken the helm.

As a youth, growing up in the Tampa Bay area of Florida, I spent many days sailing with my father, who was an avid sailor. He loved being on the water. It was on Tampa Bay where I learned the ways of the water and the keys to navigation.

When moving from point to point on the open water, one must consider several factors to successfully guide the vessel from point A to point B, including wind direction and speed, water conditions (wave heights), sail settings, and the direction of the vessel.

Among the many facets of sailing, the sailor must always be cognizant of the conditions, for wind can be fickle in direction and speed. Sailing conditions require a nimbleness of approach and flexibility of sorts, for the sailor may have some control over the boat, but has very little control over the boating conditions. Understanding present conditions is imperative to ably and successfully navigate the sailboat. In short, navigating a sailboat is somewhat of an art form.

As we interact with our culture and the people in it, we are much like the captain of a boat, navigating adeptly as witnesses for Jesus. As individuals and as the church we need to understand our present cultural conditions. But unlike the sailor, who must understand the prevailing winds, followers of Jesus must understand prevailing beliefs. And when we do, we will be better equipped to provide a humble, respectful and effective witness for Christ.

Just as the sons of Issachar "had understanding of the times, to know what Israel ought to do" (1 Chronicles 12:32), we need to understand our present time in order to know how we can most effectively be salt and light in our culture.

In short, knowing what's going on helps our going out. While true in sailing, it's also true in living out our faith amid the spiritual gale.

In the spiritual, understanding the times in which we live, like the sons of Issachar, is critical. But there's much more than just increased persecution, hostility, and opposition in our country. There's a changing spiritual landscape.

Contextualization involves an attempt to present the gospel in a culturally relevant way, so those we relate to can connect with the gospel and person of Jesus.

Interestingly, the gospel message, the person and work of Jesus, and the truth of God's Word are transcendent, yet the way we communicate with our audience may differ. Understanding our mission field will help inform our witness and make our testimony more germane.

James Emory White noted:

> "The message of the gospel is unchanging; the method of communicating that gospel must change according to the language, culture and background of the audience. We never want to abuse this or cross a line. The goal is to be in the world, not of it. But we are to be out there on the front lines communicating the gospel in the most compelling, culturally relevant and understandable way possible." [29]

The Apostle Paul, our primary example of contextualizing the gospel, wrote: "I have become all things to all men, that I might by all means save some." (1 Corinthians 9:22)

Paul desired to share the gospel in culturally relevant ways. In other words, he desired to share the gospel in a way his audience could understand. Paul contextualized without compromising the gospel.

After we see Paul effectively share the gospel in a first century context, we'll briefly introduce our current cultural climate and the prevailing winds of belief blowing through it. Then we'll touch upon some simple approaches to give a "word aptly spoken." We want to "always be ready to give an answer for the reason for hope within us, with gentleness and respect" (1 Peter 3:15).

To reiterate, understanding what's going on in the culture will aid our witness as we go out into the culture as His ambassadors of reconciliation.

Paul—A First Century Example

To the Jewish People—Jews were Paul's primary audience in Acts 13:13-52. In Acts 13:14 when Paul and his companions arrived in Pisidian Antioch, they went to the synagogue on the Sabbath. Now we pick it up in verses 15-16:

> And after the reading of the Law and the Prophets, the rulers of the synagogue sent to them, saying, "Men and brethren, if you have any word of exhortation for the people, say on."
>
> Then Paul stood up, and motioning with his hand said, "Men of Israel, and you who fear God, listen:

The first lesson in contextualization is to understand your audience. Whether you're talking to a stranger or have a closer connection, it's always helpful to understand their "God-paradigm." This will inform your witness.

In this case, Paul obviously knew his audience well. He had been a "Hebrew of the Hebrews and a Pharisee" (Philippians 3:5).

In Acts 13:17-23, Paul began by sharing some of God's relationship with Israel in the Old Testament, then culminated with his testimony that Jesus was Savior and the promised Messiah of Israel (Acts 13:23).

In Acts 13:24-25, Paul refers to the testimony of John the Baptist, whom the Jewish people would have known about.

Paul makes the connection by starting with the history of God's dealings with Israel. He then connects God's promises regarding Messiah with the claim that Jesus was the fulfillment of those promises, using the Hebrew scriptures (Old Testament).

This may be stating the obvious, yet it must be stated. To communicate the gospel without compromise, we must clearly communicate the gospel.

And this is exactly what Paul does in Acts 13:26-41. He talks about the message of salvation (verse 26), the rejection and death of Messiah Jesus as foretold in the Scriptures (verses 27-29), the resurrection of Jesus (verses 30-37), and the exhortation to receive forgiveness of sins through faith in Him (verses 38-41).

When sharing the gospel, be ready for any response. With this mindset, you'll be prepared for complete acceptance or utter rejection of your witness, and everything in between. In this narrative, Paul witnessed both salvation and rejection of the message, all the while experiencing the joy of the Lord.

In Acts 13:42-43, many of the Jewish people and "God-fearing proselytes" (Gentile converts to Judaism) encouraged Paul and Barnabas to "continue in the grace of God" (Acts 13:43).

The next Sabbath we gaze upon the polarizing nature of the gospel, as Jewish people fight against the gospel, while many Gentiles embrace the message and believe (Acts 13:44-49).

As Paul and Barnabas are driven out of the district (Acts 13:50-51), they move on to Iconium with joy in their hearts: "And the disciples were filled with joy and with the Holy Spirit" (Acts 13:51).

As I ponder my Christian experience, I have experienced the great joy in simply being a vessel of God's grace in delivering the most important message—the gospel message. We can't, and don't, control the response, but we can and should be joyful in communicating the gospel and providing people the opportunity to respond, even if that response is outright rejection.

To the Gentiles—The Scene: The Areopagus in Athens. The word "Areopagus" means the "Rock of Ares" in the city and was a center of temples, cultural facilities, and a high court.

Earlier, when Paul entered the city, "his spirit was provoked within him when he saw that the city was given over to idols" (Acts 17:16). Now Epicurean and Stoic philosophers conversed with Paul:

> Then certain Epicurean and Stoic philosophers encountered him. And some said, "What does this babbler want to say?" Others said, "He seems to be a proclaimer of foreign gods," because he preached to them Jesus and the resurrection. And they took him and brought him to the Areopagus, saying, "May we know what this new doctrine is of which you speak? For you are bringing some strange things to our ears. Therefore we want to know what these things mean." For all the Athenians and the foreigners who were there spent their time in nothing else but either to tell or to hear some new thing" (Acts 17:18-21).

Epicureans believed pleasure was the greatest good, but the way to attain such pleasure was to live modestly and to gain knowledge of the workings of the world and the limits of one's desires. Epicureanism emphasized the neutrality of the gods, that they do not interfere with human lives. Stoicism taught human virtue in accord with nature was the way to happiness. Stoicism equated God with the totality of the universe (pantheism), which was contrary to Christianity. Additionally, Stoicism did not posit a beginning or end to the universe.

Though these philosophies differed greatly from the doctrines of Christianity, Paul's audience is curious about his message, despite its perplexing character. Paul, being a Roman citizen, a learned man, and God's chosen apostle to bring the gospel to the nations (Gentiles), would have understood this particular audience.

Again, understanding our audience informs our witness. Paul contextualized the gospel, by initially connecting with his audience:

> Then Paul stood in the midst of the Areopagus and said, "Men of Athens, I perceive that in all things you are very religious; for as I was passing through and considering the objects of your worship, I even found an altar with this inscription:
>
> TO THE UNKNOWN GOD
>
> Therefore, the One whom you worship without knowing, Him I proclaim to you: God, who made the world and everything in it, since He is Lord of heaven and earth, does not dwell in temples made with hands. Nor is He worshiped with men's hands, as though He needed anything, since He gives to all life, breath, and all things. And He has made from one blood every nation of men to dwell on all the face of the earth, and has determined their pre-appointed times and the boundaries of their dwellings, so that they should seek the Lord, in the hope that they might grope for Him and find Him, though He is not far from each one of us; for in Him we live and move and have our being, as also some of your own poets have said, 'For we are also His offspring' (Acts 17:22-28).

These people at the Areopagus knew little about the Scriptures—specific revelation. So instead, Paul begins by arguing for a creator through general revelation. Notice, Paul affirms points of connection while also communicating points of distinction. For example, He connects by proclaiming to them "The Unknown God," while distinguishing that He is Creator, rather than something "made with hands."

This connecting of the dots for his audience is a rational argument in contrast with the scriptural argument he used in the synagogues. For us, connecting with our audience takes time and practice. Paul is a tremendous example of how it is done.

Paul concluded his argument by presenting Christ, the resurrection, and the need for repentance:

"Therefore, since we are the offspring of God, we ought not to think that the Divine Nature is like gold or silver or stone, something shaped by art and man's devising. Truly, these times of ignorance God overlooked, but now *commands all men everywhere to repent, because He has appointed a day on which He will judge the world in righteousness by the Man whom He has ordained. He has given assurance of this to all by raising Him from the dead*" (Acts 17:29-31, italics mine).

Paul, in no uncertain terms, proclaimed Jesus, the resurrection, judgment, and the need for repentance. Clear and direct. Paul contextualized the gospel without compromising it.

As we've stated, be prepared for any response and you won't be caught off guard. The book of Acts certainly corroborates this phenomenon.

Notice in Acts 17:33-34 the response to Paul's proclamation here at Mars Hill:

And when they heard of the resurrection of the dead, some mocked, while others said, "We will hear you again on this matter." So Paul departed from among them. However, some men joined him and believed, among them Dionysius the Areopagite, a woman named Damaris, and others with them.

Some mocked. Some believed. Some remained curious. The important thing for Paul was to be faithful in sowing and watering while leaving the results to God (1 Corinthians 3:6–7).

We need to contextualize the gospel without compromise, seeking to understand and connect with our audience. We do this for the glory of Jesus and for the building of His Kingdom.

Post-Modernism: A Present, Pervasive, Cultural Condition

Years ago, I was having a conversation with a friend about absolute truth. He made a classic postmodern statement that gave me an opening. He said, "I don't believe in absolutes. I'm a relativist." I kindly responded, "Is that an absolute statement?" Silence.

This wasn't a gotcha moment. I simply wanted my friend to see a contradiction in his worldview. Yes, truth exposes error and the truth sets people free.

For our purposes, this is only a brief introduction to a massive social construct that dominates our culture. Study more on your own, but know that among unbelievers, this general worldview pervades our society. So it will serve us well to understand it better. This understanding will help us more effectively interact with those holding to its tenets.

In simplest terms, post-modernism is a complex and abstract worldview which holds that people are simply products of their social setting or culture. "Truths" are mental constructs of individuals rooted in their own cultural setting. Therefore values are individually based upon those same cultural paradigms—the implication being there are no universal values. In essence, the postmodern person creates his or her own sense of reality.

To better understand the concept of post-modernism, it will be helpful to understand how we got here from there, so to speak. So let's go back and briefly unpack the concepts of "pre-modernism" and "modernism" in order to better contextualize this recently developed worldview.

<u>Pre-Modernism</u>: Before the 1600s, people in the West generally believed that God (or the transcendent/supernatural realm) furnished the basis for moral absolutes, rationality, human dignity, and truth. This was the lens through which one could properly interpret reality and human experience. By having faith in God, the world could be rightly understood.

In short, *pre-modernism held that there is absolute truth and God is the author and revealer of that truth.* This was the predominant view in the world until the Age of Enlightenment.

<u>Modernism (1650s–1950s)</u>: Modernism held that morality, human dignity, truth, and reason rest on foundations other than God (reason, science, race, etc.). Philosopher René Descartes (1596–1650), also a Roman Catholic, famously coined the phrase, "I think, therefore I am." His skepticism of Christian dogma (i.e. a pre-modern

view of truth) and church authority removed God from center stage, replacing it with human reason as the starting point. His paradigm shift regarding truth reflected the beliefs of many people as the rationalism of the European Enlightenment (c. 1650–1800) came to the fore. Science now became the source for truth and reality, not God. During this period, religion and morality were arbitrarily demoted to the subjective realm.

In simple terms, modernism held that there was absolute truth, but it now could be discovered with certainty through observation and reason.

Post-Modernism (1950s–present): Post-modernism holds that there is no single defining source for truth and reality beyond the individual. Post-modernism simply radicalized relativism and individualism, then applied them to all spheres of knowledge—even science. For example, the idea that 2 + 2 = 4 is debatable. Really? Really. A google search of "2 + 2 doesn't equal 4" rendered over 200 million results!

In a post-modern world, truth and reality are understood to be individually shaped by personal history, social class, gender, culture, and religion. In other words, you have your truth, I have my truth, and Benny has his truth. Are you starting to see the confusion this context for truth creates?

Since truth is relative—tolerance, freedom of expression, inclusion, and refusal to claim to have the answers are the only universal values. To claim any absolutes is in direct conflict with the postmodern paradigm.

Therefore, when no universal foundation for truth, morality, or human dignity exists, you get chaos and pandemonium. And that's exactly what we see happening around the globe and in the United States today.

Does the Bible shed any light on the postmodern worldview? Yes, in that we can identify error only when measured against truth—our objective measure of reality found in God's Word. The Bible is the blueprint for reality:

"Thy Word is truth" (John 17:17).

"Jesus said to him, 'I am the way, and the truth, and the life. No one comes to the Father except through me'" (John 14:6).

"See to it that no one takes you captive by philosophy and empty deceit, according to human tradition, according to the elemental spirits of the world, and not according to Christ" (Colossians 2:18).

How does postmodernism answer the four foundational questions whereby we can objectively measure a worldview? In simple terms, this way:

Where did we come from? No one can say, since there are no absolutes.

How does Postmodernism provide meaning? As the saying goes, beauty is in the eye of the beholder. Even so, in postmodernism the meaning of life or meaning in life is ascribed by the individual. It is subjective and arbitrary.

What moral framework does postmodernism provide? Again, any moral framework is arbitrary and subjective.

What is our ultimate destiny? As with origins, postmodernism says, "Who can know?" Not very hopeful.

In light of an increasing number of people in America embracing this paradigm, how then shall we engage the postmodernist in our individual spheres of influence?

> "For the weapons of our warfare are not carnal but mighty in God for pulling down strongholds, casting down arguments and every high thing that exalts itself against the knowledge of God" (2 Corinthians 10:4–5).

Specifically, one weapon is the "Sword of the Spirit" (Ephesians 6:17), the Word of God. We need to lovingly confront error with truth, because the truth of God's Word is a most powerful weapon.

Andrei Sakharov was a Russian nuclear physicist, anti-Soviet dissident and human rights activist. He became renowned as the designer of the Soviet Union's "Third Idea," a codename for Soviet development of thermonuclear weapons. Sakharov was an advocate of civil liberties and civil reforms in the Soviet Union. He was awarded the Nobel Peace Prize in 1975.

The man who gave the Soviet Union the bomb, stated late in his life, "The most powerful weapon in the world is the truth."[30]

No doubt, as we share the truth in love, it is good to understand our audience and communicate in a manner they can understand, as Paul did, for example, in Synagogues and at Mars Hill.

And if the gospel is rejected by the postmodernist, it's not because they can say we're wrong—there is no right or wrong in postmodern thought—rather because the message claims to be "the truth."

Jesus said, "You shall know the truth and the truth will set you free" (John 8:32).

As we share truth of Jesus and His saving work with the postmodernist, pray the Holy Spirit, the Spirit of truth, would do the work of illumination and conviction, to the end that they would be delivered from error and brought to a knowledge of He who is the Truth—the Lord Jesus.

A Growing Cultural And Religious Phenomenon

As we noted earlier, "The Times They Are A-Changin," penned over fifty years ago by Bob Dylan, was "a song with a purpose," said by Dylan himself years later. The tumultuous 60s included such cultural and societal tsunamis as the civil rights movement, the Vietnam war, and the sexual revolution.

Fast forward over fifty years later to this day—"Oh, the times, they are still a-changin." Can I get an amen?

We could point to some obvious current flash points of change such as the technological revolution, political chaos and pandemonium, or the battle over gender identity.

But there is another societal tsunami that has arisen in recent years, a massive change that is very germane to our walk with Christ and witness for Him. What is it, you may wonder?

It is called the "rise of the nones."

Who are the "nones?" They are the religiously unaffiliated,

identifying when asked to note religious affiliation—"none."

According to a 2017 Pew Research Study on Religion, roughly 25% of Americans identify themselves as "nones." That's one out of four people. This is a stark increase from 2007, the last time a similar Pew Research study was conducted, when 16% of Americans were "nones."

In numerical terms, the "nones" comprise roughly 80 million Americans and that number is rising daily. In fact, as a religious constituency, they are the fastest-growing and now second-largest religious sub-group in the United States.

As Pastor and author James Emory White notes, "The first task of any good missionary is to go to school on who it is they are trying to reach."[31] For believers living in America, our mission field includes this ever-expanding group called the "nones."

In this introduction to the "nones" and how to begin reaching them, two trends standout:

1. <u>The under-thirty group makes up the highest proportion of the "nones."</u> One-third of Americans under thirty say they have no religious affiliation. And of this group, a significant percentage have never attended church, at least on any regular basis. And this sub-group is growing. This means we must assume people know nothing about Jesus, the Bible, and the Christian faith. Rather, we must ask leading questions, allowing people to reveal their understanding and beliefs about Christianity before making proclamations. For example, "If I say one must trust in Jesus to be saved," someone identifying as a "none" may not know what "saved" means. They may not even know what it means to trust in Jesus. Therefore, assume nothing, encourage people to share so you can learn about them, and tread slowly.

2. <u>They're not necessarily atheist.</u> This is crucial and may be surprising, but the largest portion of nones (nearly 70% percent) say they believe in God or a universal spirit. In fact, some of these precious people believe in Christ on some-level, or in "Christ-consciousness." For example, if you were to ask someone if they had any kind of religious tradition growing up, a person identifying as a "none" may say they never went to church growing up or that their

family wasn't at all religious (perhaps their parents also were 'nones'). The application for us as His witnesses is to recognize that despite this fact, we should not assume that the individual doesn't have spiritual leanings or interests.

Rather, we should ask, "Do you have any personal spiritual convictions or interests?" Based on the statistics, most will say yes. Allow them to elaborate so you can gather information.

Engaging the Political/Social Barrier

This barrier is personal. Since the "nones" tend to hold unbiblical moral views like being pro-choice and for homosexual marriage, contrarian views will create a built-in barrier to communication, even that which pertains to spiritual matters.

How do we therefore build personal bridges with those who may also stereotype Christians as homophobes, bigoted, and narrow-minded? Well, we should seek to move their perception from negative to positive or at least neutral. And how do we accomplish this?

In a word, love—*agape* love, the love of God. As we present an authentic and loving testimony for Christ in word and deed, may we gain a voice with those we're striving to reach with the gospel.

Ultimately, the gospel is about Jesus and His love. It is about breaking down the greatest barrier, the barrier between God and man—sin—through His death and resurrection on our behalf. Jesus is about meeting man's greatest need, the need to be forgiven. The love of God found in Christ transcends political/social barriers and goes to the heart of the matter: the spiritual barrier between God and man.

Engaging the Institutional Barrier

The "nones" are not rejecting God, they're rejecting institutional religion. The Pew Study on Religion found that while nearly 70% percent of "nones" say they believe in God or a universal spirit, a similar percentage believe religious institutions are too concerned with money and power.

How do we build bridges to spiritual conversations in spite of such a barrier? We make the issue of Jesus personal, not institutional. With God's wisdom, discernment, along with tact and love, we share that while institutional abuse of money and power do have some legitimacy, the ultimate issue is personal: Who is Jesus?

It's okay to agree that the institution of the church has issues (because it does), but at the same time we point out that if Jesus is who He claims to be, shouldn't we then follow Him?

Because Christianity at its core is about Jesus and knowing Him. Therefore we need to show them the love of God and tell them about the person and work of Jesus, which are in sharp contrast to the control, manipulation and power of some institutional religion.

Engaging the Post-Modern Barrier

When it comes to content, dogma, orthodoxy—anything "spelled out" or offering a "system of beliefs"—the general position of the "nones" who believe in God or a universal spirit is: "Who knows?" Sound post-modern? You betcha.

But that's not all. When asked about specific beliefs, they're very content with "nothing in particular." According to the recent Pew Survey on Religion, among the "nones" who say they believe "nothing in particular," 88% also say they are not even looking for a specific faith or religion.

In basic terms, post-modern thought as it relates to truth espouses that there may or may not be truth, but who can know? We see this paradigm reflected in the non-committal and very undogmatic spiritual positions of the "nones."

Considering this basic reality, how then do we engage this barrier and build bridges to present the distinct and unique claim that Jesus is the way, the truth and the life—the only way to God?

We need to be more processional and less presentational in our witness. Evangelism is a process—it takes time [see the Parable of the Soils in Matthew 13:1-8, 18-23].

The "nones," just as with others possessing post-modern views, are less interested in *presentations* of the gospel and more interested in *conversations* about the gospel. We should therefore take a long-term view and leave that person with the desire to continue conversing about spiritual matters.

The Apologetic See-Saw

While we as followers of Jesus are sometimes challenged to defend our faith, we should "always be ready to give an answer ... with gentleness and respect" (1 Peter 3:15). Healthy dialogue and discussion should be two-way, so it's also appropriate at times to ask why another believes what they believe and what is the ultimate consequence of their belief.

Sometimes, as people are challenged to grapple with these questions, doubt in their own beliefs arises and becomes a powerful tool in their conversion to Christ. The Holy Spirit, at times, can and does use a person's doubt in their existing belief system to reveal that Jesus is the way, the truth, and the life; that He died for our sins and rose again the third day so that we, through faith in Him, might be forgiven, reconciled to God, and experience abundant and eternal life.

A simple way to be on offense without being offensive is to ask someone regarding their faith system, "Why do you believe what you believe?"

A poignant follow-up is, "What is the ultimate destination your belief takes you to and why?"

When people have difficulty defending their own positions and see problems with them, a rejection of their own positions may arise creating a void. And what will fill the void? Hopefully the truth.

Challenging people takes wisdom and discernment. How we challenge them should be with an attitude of gentleness and respect. Yet there is a time and place when it's right and good. As we walk by faith, the Lord will guide us.

May we go forth into our individual spheres of influence—where each of us works, lives, and plays—increasingly aware that they are in our midst—namely "nones." And by God's grace and through the power of the Holy Spirit, may we be the ministers of reconciliation He's called us to be—to the end that many who are "none" may be won to Christ.

A Final Navigational Alert

As we seek to navigate the cultural waters, being salt and light amidst many caught up in the cultural drift, the only way to contextualize the gospel for someone is to know that someone. And the more we listen, the more we learn. Interestingly, as we listen to and learn about someone's viewpoints, including those about spiritual matters, we affirm them. In listening, we in so many words are communicating, "I care about what you think." And this position stands in stark contrast to this view that many unbelievers have of Christians, which is, "You Christians only want to be heard."

So, go forth, listening, learning, and loving, relationally navigating towards understanding others and contextualizing the gospel for them…to the end that many would be saved.

Chapter 7

Picking Your Battles

I remember the moment like it was yesterday, but this was no scene from a painful movie—this was real life. The pall of gloom settled over the gas station as long lines of impatient people waited to fill up cars and escape the impending nightmare.

It was August 1992. I was visiting my maternal grandmother, Nanny Lillian, with my mom and stepfather. We had made the trek across the state, leaving St. Petersburg and arriving in North Miami Beach on Thursday afternoon for a routine family visit.

On the afternoon of our arrival, I recall looking at the weather report on television—the named cyclone—Andrew—was a weak tropical storm. Further strengthening was questionable. Oh, what a difference two days can make.

By Saturday afternoon a mandatory evacuation order had been given for North Miami Beach and other areas. Andrew had intensified into a major hurricane and was bearing down on the Florida coast, soon to strike.

After getting my grandmother to safer ground inland (where she remained safe through the storm), my mother, stepfather, and I raced across the state to our home in Treasure Island, located in west Central Florida, where we would ride the storm out, escaping the worst of the hurricane.

Andrew was a Category 5 hurricane with maximum sustained winds of over 150 mph when it struck South Florida. It was the most destructive hurricane in Florida's history. The storm was also ranked as the costliest hurricane in United States history until being surpassed by Katrina in 2005 along with Harvey and Irma in 2017.

It should go without saying, but when a storm is packing 150 mph winds, there is no decision whether one should ignore evacuation orders and remain in the path of a meteorological monster like Andrew.

But growing up on the coast of west Central Florida, there were times a tropical storm approached our area and we had a choice. When battling mother nature, it is prudent to pick your battles wisely, for life and death can hang in the balance. In the case of Hurricane Andrew, that was an easy decision—hit the road Jack—which is literally what we did—as my stepfather's name was...yes—Jack. And my mom, just as recently as 2017, evacuated the Tampa Bay area during Hurricane Irma, riding the storm out in Atlanta, rather than taking on that life-threatening tempest.

It may seem counterintuitive, but in the spiritual arena, as it relates to our walk with God in seeking to fulfill the Great Commission, there are also times to pick our battles.

We are in the midst of a storm of sorts—a spiritual war. And there are times in fact, when we are faced with decisions—decisions whether to engage a person or situation, or flee.

And interestingly, there are times when the Lord Himself will prevent us from heading into an individual gale. At other times, we need wisdom and discernment in knowing when to move into a situation or move away from it.

Our first century brethren provide instructional examples that will help us navigate the current tempest that is present day America.

When God Says Don't Go

Frenetic meets confusion and chaos. Speed dating? No. Rather, the afternoon rush hour on the lower East Side of Manhattan, New York City. I was walking around trying to find a particular apartment building, as I had an appointment with a Jewish man to share the gospel. For six years (2003-2009) the core of my ministry was one-on-one visitation with Jewish men, sharing the gospel, or discipling new Jewish believers.

The initial meeting was not going well. To be honest, it wasn't going at all. The lower east side of Manhattan is made up primarily of immigrants. I couldn't find anyone on the street who spoke English to ask directions of. I couldn't hale a cab, as it was the time of day when cabbies in the city were changing shifts. I had an address and a phone number, but the man I was scheduled to meet with couldn't give me proper directions. I was a bit disoriented and didn't know my exact location. I was also more than a bit frustrated. And by the way, this was before the advent of smart phones. My cell phone at the time, what we might call a dumb phone today, didn't have GPS.

After perhaps thirty minutes of wandering, I called off the search. Most of Manhattan is on a grid—simple to navigate. But the lower east side isn't quite so simple. On this day, the area was kind of like the Bermuda Triangle and I was its latest victim.

I never made it to that appointment. In fact, that initial visit with this particular Jewish man never happened.

Could there have been more to this incident than meets the eye? Is it possible there was some kind of Divine intervention in this bizarre and singular experience? Could it have been that the Lord was forbidding me to go?

Acts 16 includes a very interesting passage where the Lord says, in essence, "No, don't go." Moreover, He forbid Paul and Timothy from going and ministering as they had desired. As we seek understanding, perhaps there's a lesson for us.

Earlier in Acts 16, as Paul begins his second missionary journey, he meets Timothy for the first time while in the city of Lystra. Timothy joined Paul and Silas in the work of the gospel. In Acts 16:5, we see God blessing the ministry as "churches were strengthened in the faith, and increased in number daily."

As they continue their journey, they are now forbidden by God to minister in Asia: "Now when they had gone through Phrygia and the region of Galatia, they were forbidden by the Holy Spirit to preach the word in Asia" (Acts 16:6).

Why does God forbid them? And more so, *how* does He forbid them? We don't know. Luke doesn't tell us. At this point I'm reminded of the Apostle Paul's words from 2 Corinthians 5:7, "For we walk by faith, not by sight." Walking with the Lord is a faith journey. And the Lord, in His providence and sovereignty, has the prerogative to guide, lead, and even forbid without explanation.

As Paul, Silas, and Timothy continue, they are once again stonewalled by the Lord: "After they had come to Mysia, they tried to go into Bithynia, but the Spirit did not permit them" (Acts 16:7).

Here we get a bit more information about the team's intention. I wonder how they tried, how the Spirit stopped them, and why. And again, Luke doesn't divulge an explanation.

Proverbs 16:9 is one of my life verses, which I find applicable to this situation and perhaps to that strange afternoon years ago on the lower east side of Manhattan: "In his heart a man plans his course, but the Lord determines his steps" (NIV, 1984 ed.).

Paul's team had felt compelled to go into Bithynia and tried to go, yet were not permitted. I wonder if in spite of my desire to visit that Jewish man years ago, if it was the Holy Spirit who did not permit me. I don't know for sure, but I suppose Paul, Silas, and Timothy didn't get lost along the way and simply give up. "Can anyone tell me how to get to Bithynia?" was probably not part of the conversation.

Ministry, like life, has a way of moving us along. And that's precisely what Paul's team did. We again see the hand of God intervening and orchestrating events:

> So passing by Mysia, they came down to Troas. And a vision appeared to Paul in the night. A man of Macedonia stood and pleaded with him, saying, "Come over to Macedonia and help us." Now after he had seen the vision, immediately we sought to go to Macedonia, concluding that the Lord had called us to preach the gospel to them (Acts 16:8-10).

Some doors close. Others open. And it is God who is Lord over all. In fact, history is His story. The Lord orchestrates all the events of history in order to accomplish His perfect will. What may appear to be chaos and pandemonium to us is not to God. He has it all under control.

When our efforts appear to not be working, remember that God is always working. In fact, the will of God is always at work.

"Remember this, and show yourselves men; Recall to mind, O you transgressors. Remember the former things of old, For I am God, and there is no other; I am God, and there is none like Me, declaring the end from the beginning, And from ancient times things that are not yet done, Saying, *'My counsel shall stand, And I will do all My pleasure'*" (Isaiah 46:8-10, italics mine).

It was God's pleasure to move Paul, Silas, and Timothy to Macedonia, where they had a divine appointment with Lydia. She and her household came to faith.

What may appear to be interruptions or disruptions may be the Lord's way of redirecting our paths to accomplish His will. I don't know how Paul and team reacted when they were stonewalled by the Spirit, but I can tell you I was not happy at all with the events of that surreal afternoon years ago on the lower east side.

Saying yes to God's no takes faith. And what this looks like in our lives may be different in application, yet is the same in principle. As you strive to reach others with the gospel, be flexible, seeking God's best, allowing Him to close doors and redirect your paths.

A Time To Move On

The Christian walk is a walk of faith. And so is the process of sharing our faith. There are times in the providence of God when doors of opportunity open and times when doors that were once open close.

As we've discussed, God hasn't called us to check out from living in the midst of increasing persecution. Just the opposite. He desires that we walk "...blameless and harmless, children of God without fault in the midst of a crooked and perverse generation, among whom you shine as lights in the world" (Philippians 2:15).

"To everything there is a season, a time for every purpose under heaven." For "He has made everything beautiful in its time" (Ecclesiastes 3:1, 11). This includes "A time to keep silence, and a time to speak" (Ecclesiastes 3:7b). Additionally, there is a time to move into a situation and a time to move on from a situation.

As we journey through life, people will enter our lives and doors of opportunity will open for us to sow and water gospel seeds. And then, at future points in time, those same doors that once were open will close, windows of opportunity will fade, and a season of sowing and watering ends. Have you been there?

I certainly have.

And what ought our response be to such circumstances? Move on.

But isn't that difficult and sometimes painful? I've invested time, energy, and prayer in the lives of various people. There were times of demonstrating God's love and other times I had the opportunity to proclaim the wonders of His love found in the gospel.

And then that person exited my life. It may be they move away. It may be they no longer want to hang out with the Jesus freak. Had I been overbearing (my thoughts, not theirs)? It could be a natural or an abrupt conclusion. In any case, they are removed from my life and I'm left to simply move on.

Have you been there?

I certainly have.

Again, let's turn our attention to the Apostle Paul and examine the circumstances surrounding his moving on as found in Acts 17. And though the circumstances surrounding his moving on are unique, perhaps there are some principles we can draw from his experience that can inform and encourage our witness.

While Paul and Silas continued ministry during Paul's second missionary journey, their travels took them to Thessalonica, where Paul taught for three weeks. While there, the ministry was fruitful:

> Now when they had passed through Amphipolis and Apollonia, they came to Thessalonica, where there was a synagogue of the Jews. Then Paul, as his custom was, went in to them, and for three Sabbaths reasoned with them from the

Scriptures, explaining and demonstrating that the Christ had to suffer and rise again from the dead, and saying, "This Jesus whom I preach to you is the Christ." And some of them were persuaded; and a great multitude of the devout Greeks, and not a few of the leading women, joined Paul and Silas (Acts 17:1-4).

So far, so good. The fruit of salvation bloomed. Trouble, however, was not far away. A group of Jews in Thessalonica opposed the gospel, and that opposition became violent:

But the Jews who were not persuaded, becoming envious, took some of the evil men from the marketplace, and gathering a mob, set all the city in an uproar and attacked the house of Jason, and sought to bring them out to the people. But when they did not find them, they dragged Jason and some brethren to the rulers of the city, crying out, "These who have turned the world upside down have come here too. Jason has harbored them, and these are all acting contrary to the decrees of Caesar, saying there is another king—Jesus." And they troubled the crowd and the rulers of the city when they heard these things. So when they had taken security from Jason and the rest, they let them go (Acts 17:5-9).

The security mentioned in the passage was a pledge or bond which would be forfeited by Jason if Paul and his companions continued to share the gospel. Claiming another king but Caesar was a serious crime.

Though a church had been born in Thessalonica, Paul, Timothy, and Silas immediately left town and fled to Berea, a town fifty miles west of Thessalonica. When they arrived, they continued their work and once again saw fruit. As before, trouble followed. Rabble-rousers followed them all the way from Thessalonica. This time, however, only Paul left town. Silas and Timothy remained, but only briefly, as Paul would command they join him in Athens.

> Then the brethren immediately sent Paul and Silas away by night to Berea. When they arrived, they went into the synagogue of the Jews. These were more fair-minded than those in Thessalonica, in that they received the word with all readiness, and searched the Scriptures daily to find out whether these things were so. Therefore many of them believed, and also not a few of the Greeks, prominent women as well as men. But when the Jews from Thessalonica learned that the word of God was preached by Paul at Berea, they came there also and stirred up the crowds. Then immediately the brethren sent Paul away, to go to the sea; but both Silas and Timothy remained there. So those who conducted Paul brought him to Athens; and receiving a command for Silas and Timothy to come to him with all speed, they departed (Acts 17:10-15).

In the case of Paul, Silas, and Timothy, the time to move on was quite clear. Although they left, the Spirit of God remained, as did those who had believed.

In our lives moving on generally won't involve such hostile circumstances. But as the headlines warrant, we understand our culture is increasingly opposed to our Christian witness. And for some of us, this storm of opposition is personal. Yes, there are times people with whom we have shared the gospel will exit our lives for various reasons. And there are times the Lord may call us to stop ministering to someone in our life, according to His plans.

I've noticed in my own Christian journey it's easier for me to understand why someone has exited my life. However, I find it more difficult to know when to "cut someone loose," so to speak.

There are no easy answers in this instance. We walk by faith and must trust the Lord's leading in all areas, including this area of moving on.

Whether we move in or move on, we should seek to move in line with the Lord according to His will. To that end, here are a few Scriptures pertaining to God's guidance to light our way:

Psalm 16:7-8. "I will bless the Lord who has given me counsel; My heart also instructs me in the night seasons. I have set the Lord always before me; Because He is at my right hand I shall not be moved."

Psalm 25:4-5. "Show me Your ways, O Lord; Teach me Your paths. Lead me in Your truth and teach me, For You are the God of my salvation; On You I wait all the day."

Psalm 32:8-9. "I will instruct you and teach you in the way you should go; I will guide you with My eye. Do not be like the horse or like the mule, Which have no understanding, Which must be harnessed with bit and bridle, Else they will not come near you."

Proverbs 3:5-6. "Trust in the Lord with all your heart, And lean not on your own understanding; In all your ways acknowledge Him, And He shall direct your paths."

James 1:5. "If any of you lacks wisdom, let him ask of God, who gives to all liberally and without reproach, and it will be given to him."

As we follow the Lord, may He give each one of us greater wisdom and discernment as people come into our lives and when the Lord calls us to move on. And may we praise and thank God for the time He does allow us to sow and water gospel seeds into the hearts of the people we encounter until they may exit our lives.

As you reflect upon these lessons, there are perhaps situations and people that represent a storm of sorts as it relates to your witness. Whether the Lord is leading you to sail headlong into the storm or evacuate, praise and thank Him. Whether to move in, move away, or move on we can trust the Lord, seeking His guidance in any circumstance we find ourselves. Our Heavenly Father knows best.

Chapter 8

God Gives The Increase

Have you ever looked outside on a windy day and seen "helicopter" seeds spinning through the air? Or picked up a dandelion and blown on it, sending the tiny, fluffy seeds flying all over the place? Wind is very important for dispersing seeds to help plants reproduce.

Like an endless army of parachutists released from an airplane, "winged" seeds travel the wind currents and gentle breezes of the earth, possibly colonizing a distant mountain slope or fertile valley. Literally hundreds of species in many plant families have this remarkable method of dispersal. To utilize this "blowing in the wind" method is, well, mind-blowing. Some of the ingenious adaptations for this method of wind dispersal include seeds that resemble parachutes, helicopters and gliders.

> "One astronomer once observed a strange formation of flying objects through his telescope. He was focusing on a squadron of tiny parachute seeds high above his house. And the entire plant body of wolffia (the world's smallest flowering plant) may be transported by powerful cyclonic storms. In the southeastern United States there are records of wolffia plant bodies less than one millimeter long being carried by a tornado, and they have even been reported in the water of melted hailstones." [32]

In the spiritual, you and I are the vessels of God's grace as we plant Kingdom seeds throughout the world. Jesus described the Kingdom in many ways including: "The kingdom of God is as if a man should scatter seed on the ground" (Matthew 4:26). As we think of seed sowing, the Holy Spirit is the wind that disperses the seeds of the Kingdom—prayer, good works, and good words—through the sower. And you thought you couldn't fly.

This is a fantastic word picture that sets up for us a very important concept. We, as His people, are called to sow seed. We're even called to water them (by the same means we sowed: prayer, good works, and proclamation), but what of the results?

The Apostle Paul summed it up: "I planted, Apollos watered, but God gave the increase. So then neither he who plants is anything, nor he who waters, but God who gives the increase" (1 Corinthians 3:6-7).

The specific kind of sowing and reaping we'll focus on in this chapter is evangelistic in nature. Certainly there are various areas of reaping and sowing in life, like moral and financial. But for our purpose, we focus on the evangelistic. This was Paul's context in 1 Corinthians 3:6-7.

In God's providence, He uses each of our lives to sow gospel seed uniquely throughout the world in a variety of ways. But the results are His doing. Our calling is simply to be faithful to sow and water as He leads and guides us.

Just as the mystery of the right combination of sun, water, and soil conditions are necessary to bear fruit in the physical world, the right conditions in the spiritual are also of God's own doing.

Also, only He truly knows the condition of the soil, that is, the human heart. So we are called to faithfulness. Leave the fruitfulness to Him. Jeremiah is a good example for us; God called him to preach repentance to ancient Israel. God told Jeremiah they wouldn't respond. Jeremiah was faithful to proclaim God's message for twenty-three years with no fruit:

> "From the thirteenth year of Josiah the son of Amon, king of Judah, even to this day, this is the twenty-third year in which the word of the Lord has come to me; and I have spoken to you, rising early and speaking, but you have not listened" (Jeremiah 25:3).

If we think some elements of our culture are challenging, cynical, skeptical, or downright obstinate regarding the things of God, then we need to remember that this is not new. So don't get discouraged with the lack of results of sowing. Seek the Lord and strive to be faithful to go, do and say as He wills.

We sow, we water, but God gives the increase. That should take the pressure off.

The gale blowing against the thrust of our Great Commission-living need not scare us or intimidate us. It should motivate us to godly living and intentional witnessing. While the culture is blowing seeds of discord, chaos, and pandemonium, the Holy Spirit is compelling us to sow seeds of His doing.

Let's first note the elements of sowing gospel seed. Then we'll examine the results, sometimes surprising in nature, of our sowing. Then we'll reiterate that it is God Who gives the increase. And finally, we'll be exhorted to keep fighting the good fight of sowing faithfully for His Kingdom sake. All of this, through the prism of our first century example—the early church.

Be A Farmer.

Sow Gospel Seed. I grew up in a condominium in Treasure Island, Florida. We were only a ten-minute drive from the beach. I loved the water and the sun. But had you told me growing up that one day I would become a spiritual farmer and that these two elements, the sun and water, would be critical to that endeavor, I would have thought you a bit off. Today I am a farmer for God—and so are you.

Jesus' parable of the soils in Luke 8:4-15 sheds light on this reality:

> And when a great multitude had gathered, and they had come to Him from every city, He spoke by a parable: "A sower went out to sow his seed. And as he sowed, some fell by the wayside; and it was trampled down, and the birds of the air devoured it. Some fell on rock; and as soon as it sprang up, it withered away because it lacked moisture. And some fell among thorns,

and the thorns sprang up with it and choked it. But others fell on good ground, sprang up, and yielded a crop a hundredfold." When He had said these things He cried, "He who has ears to hear, let him hear."

Then His disciples asked Him, saying, "What does this parable mean?" And He said, "To you it has been given to know the mysteries of the kingdom of God, but to the rest it is given in parables, that 'Seeing they may not see, And hearing they may not understand.'

"Now the parable is this: The seed is the word of God. Those by the wayside are the ones who hear; then the devil comes and takes away the word out of their hearts, lest they should believe and be saved. But the ones on the rock are those who, when they hear, receive the word with joy; and these have no root, who believe for a while and in time of temptation fall away. Now the ones that fell among thorns are those who, when they have heard, go out and are choked with cares, riches, and pleasures of life, and bring no fruit to maturity. But the ones that fell on the good ground are those who, having heard the word with a noble and good heart, keep it and bear fruit with patience.

People can't know Christ without the proclamation of the gospel, for "faith comes by hearing and hearing by the Word of God" (Romans 10:17). We're called to sow gospel seed, which is the Word of God, and that takes time. The soil is the condition of a human heart, as Jesus explained, and is where the seed lands. As one Bible commentator notes, "The soils do not represent individual moments of decision as much as a lifelong response to God's Word." [33]

Think about it in a physical sense. A farmer sows seed—that's an event. It rains one day—that's another event. The sun comes up day after day and feeds that seed—those days are individual events. It rains another day—that's an event. And so on.

The first time I heard the gospel, I was in college. My initial responses were outright rejection of that message. However, people kept coming, and the Holy Spirit kept working on my heart. Four years passed between the time people began witnessing to me in 1983 and the day I trusted in Christ in 1987.

By understanding evangelism is a process, you will gain confidence and more aptly balance the urgency of sharing Jesus while respecting people enough to give them time, space, and margins to process the truth.

Years ago, I was at Brooklyn College in New York City talking to students about Jesus. I was sharing the gospel with an orthodox Jewish student and I asked him, "Have you ever heard this message before?" Perplexed, he said, "Never in my life." He certainly needed time to process the gospel message.

We don't know the condition of a human heart and we may not know a person's previous exposure to a Christian witness. But God does. God calls us to engage and sow gospel seed, the Word of God, believing in God to do what only He can do—bless our efforts.

Sow through Good Works. As witnesses for Jesus, we can recognize and meet needs to demonstrate the love of God. In our sphere of influence, looking for ways to serve people and meet needs can be a wonderful initial engagement in the evangelistic process.

What that may look like for you is unique to your sphere of influence. What can you do? What needs do you see? With whom do you start? Well, how about with one person? We can't serve everybody, but we can serve somebody.

As we've mentioned, on a person's journey to faith, they typically will have many touch points with the gospel. Good deeds play a part in that journey.

Let's not have any illusions about attempting to sow gospel seeds into people's lives through service. Understand that there are people who won't respond the way we'd like or aren't interested in us meeting needs they may have. In Luke 17:11-17, Jesus heals ten lepers, yet only one returned to Jesus, giving thanks and glorifying God. Jesus, in His omniscience, knew only one would return, yet it didn't prevent him from healing them all nonetheless. Jesus healed them not because they would respond, but because they were broken and had a need.

Eric Swanson and Rick Rusaw, in their book *The Externally Focused Quest*, provide excellent perspective regarding good deeds and their place in our evangelistic efforts:

> Although we believe there is no more fertile ground for evangelism than selfless service, we serve not to convert but because we have been converted. We serve not to make others Christians but because we are Christians. People are worthy recipients whether they become Christ followers or not. Evangelism is our ultimate motive, but can never be our ulterior motive for serving.[34]

John Stott, regarding our motives in doing good deeds, adds:

> "To sum up, we are sent into the world, like Jesus, to serve. This is the natural expression of our love for our neighbors. We love. We go. We serve. And in this we have (or should have) no ulterior motive. True, the gospel lacks visibility if we merely preach it, and lacks credibility if we who preach it are interested in only souls and have no concern about the welfare of people's bodies, situations and communities. Yet the reason for our acceptance of social responsibility is not primarily in order to give the gospel either a visibility or a credibility it would otherwise lack, but rather simple uncomplicated compassion. Love has no need to justify itself. It merely expresses itself in service wherever it sees need."[35]

With this healthy perspective in mind, we need to always be ready, expecting God to open doors so we can share His love in word and deed. Swanson and Rusaw state, "Good deeds create goodwill, and goodwill is a wonderful platform for good conversations about the good news."[36]

Sow in Prayer. Lastly, we also sow and water through the critical means of prayer. This should go without saying. Books have been written on evangelistic prayer. And although we touch upon it, this may be the most important aspect of our sowing.

We need to bathe everything in prayer, including our evangelistic effort. In 1 Thessalonians 5:17, the apostle wrote: "Pray without ceasing." Of what was he speaking? Perhaps the ambiguity speaks of an overarching theme to always be in a spirit of prayer.

I would recommend a great website filled with biblical prayers called kingdompraying.com. Dr. Kevin Meador has done a great service for the church in providing prayers for various areas, including prayers for the lost, prayers for open doors, and more. Using Bible verses for prayer is powerful and fruitful.

Ralph Herring states:

> That Satan trembles when he sees the weakest saint upon his knees, why not make him tremble? Why not storm the very gates of hell? Nothing could please God more. In the conflict that is upon us, certainly we can ill afford to neglect one weapon Satan does not have in his arsenal and the one he fears most—prayer.[37]

Let's touch upon what to pray for based on 1 Peter 3:15, which states: "But sanctify the Lord God in your hearts, and always be ready to give a defense to everyone who asks you a reason for the hope that is in you, with meekness and fear."

A Right Heart. "But in your hearts sanctify Christ as Lord." Give Him more of your heart in this area, a heart that breaks for the lost.

Readiness. "Always be ready to give an account." Prepare to share.

A Right Spirit. "With gentleness and respect." Our witness should be a humble witness.

Additionally, among many things, we should also pray for:

Peace. "Be anxious for nothing, but in everything by prayer and supplication with thanksgiving, let your requests be made known to God and the peace of God, which surpasses understanding, will guard your hearts and minds through Christ Jesus" (Philippians 4:6-7).

Wisdom. "Walk in wisdom toward those who are outside, redeeming the time" (Colossians 4:5).

Open Doors. "Continue earnestly in prayer ... praying also for us, that God would open to us a door for the word, to speak the mystery of Christ" (Colossians 4:2-3). Ask God to give you opportunities to share the gospel with others.

The Lost. "The Lord opened [Lydia's] heart to heed the things spoken by Paul" (Acts 16:15), which we'll examine shortly. Ask God to move in the heart of those who need Him, that they would be open to hear, that they would be enabled to understand the gospel, to the end that they would believe in Jesus.

Other Witnesses. "Then He said to His disciples, 'The harvest is plentiful, but the laborers are few. Therefore pray the Lord of the harvest to send out laborers into His harvest'" (Matthew 9:35). Since evangelism is a team effort, pray God would send other believers to be salt and light to others, even among those with whom you have a direct witness.

So do the work of a farmer: sowing, watering, and laboring in your "field," the sphere of influence in which God has placed you. And develop the patience and trust of a farmer, trusting the "Lord of the Harvest" to do what only He can—change the human heart.

The Desired Results

We live in a world that often says hard work and doing the right thing will bring the desired result. To promote the desired result there are a myriad of tools at our disposal: self-help tools, user guides, how to's, the three steps to this and the four steps to that. They may come in the form of seminars, DVDs, CDs, books, television shows, and so on.

As we think about the desired results from our evangelistic sowing, it would be good for us to think in biblical terms and not according to worldly standards. Because as we explore the desired results according to God's paradigm, we will see that A+B doesn't necessarily equal C.

Let me explain.

Success in Witnessing. We all want to be successful in our witness. The best definition for success in witnessing I have found comes from Bill Bright, founder of Campus Crusade for Christ: "Success in witnessing is simply taking the initiative to share Christ in the power of the Holy Spirit, and leaving the results to God."[38]

I really like this definition, first based upon what it says, but secondly, based upon what it doesn't say.

It doesn't say success in witnessing is having somebody receive the Lord, although that is certainly the most desired result.

This idea of success in witnessing is an issue for many believers. I have heard Christians tell me they've felt like failures in their witness because they haven't led someone to Christ. I've had to comfort them, reminding them that God is the Author of Salvation and not them. Their responsibility is to be a faithful witness.

Taking the Initiative. Based upon our definition above taking the initiative to share Christ in the power of the Holy Spirit is the key to success in witnessing. In fact, this is our role in the evangelistic endeavor.

Spirit-led evangelistic activity is part of the success formula. Sharing Christ and the gospel message is central to this endeavor—and we're not alone. The Lord is with us.

What does it mean to take initiative? In part it is *to go when God calls, to go where God calls you, and to go to whom God calls you.* It may be in the context of personal relationships and it may be in the context of "witnessing on the way."

And we do all this through the power of the Spirit. We are never alone in the process. When Jesus called His disciples, He said: "Follow me and I will make you fishers of men" (Matthew 4:19).

At the end of His ministry, just before He ascended to heaven He stated, "Go and make disciples of all nations ... and I will be with you always" (Matthew 28:18-20).

And just before His ascension, Jesus said: "But you shall receive power when the Holy Spirit has come upon you; and you shall be witnesses to Me in Jerusalem, and in all Judea and Samaria, and to the end of the earth" (Acts 1:8).

What Results? The results of our evangelistic efforts are always in God's hands and the people we witness to have a choice. Whatever the results, whether painful or joyful, they are not ours to control.

This certainly flies in opposition to worldly endeavors, where success often has a positive outcome, is man-centered, and produces a desirable result. In the Kingdom of God, our faithful evangelistic effort in the power of the Holy Spirit may result in the following:

Salvation (Acts 2:1-41, Acts 10:34-48, Acts 16:25-34, and many other passages).

Arrests and threats (Acts 4:1-22, Acts 16:16-24, Acts 21:26-36).

Stoning (Acts 14:1-7, 19-20).

Assault (Acts 17:5-9)

Rioting (Acts 19:21-41)

Death (Acts 7:1-60)

These can be the results of faithful witnessing.

A biblical perspective of expectations regarding our witness reveals that most of the results are "undesirable" from a human perspective. In God's Kingdom, the desired result is initially the conviction of sin. And often, a person's initial response to conviction is typically not salvation. In fact, evangelistic research indicates that it typically takes several exposures to the gospel before a person ultimately makes the decision to receive the Lord. That was certainly my case, as my initial responses to a gospel witness were rejection of the message. And you? What was your initial response? Don't be surprised, when your faithfulness in witnessing brings about various negative responses. Understand conviction must precede confession of sin and the process of surrendering to the Lord is often just that—a process.

Being Okay With That. So, now we see the desired results, are sometimes painful. There is great blessing in identifying with the Lord in His suffering through faithful witnessing. He said:

> "Blessed are those who are persecuted for righteousness' sake, For theirs is the kingdom of heaven. "Blessed are you when they revile and persecute you, and say all kinds of evil against you falsely for My sake. Rejoice and be exceedingly glad, for great is your reward in heaven, for so they persecuted the prophets who were before you" (Matthew 5:10-12).

So strive to be successful in witnessing, and be okay with the consequences according to God. Paul said, "Rejoice always, pray without ceasing, in everything give thanks; for this is the will of God in Christ Jesus for you" (1 Thessalonians 5:16-18).

God Gives The Increase

I enjoy internet research. I find it fascinating that with a click of a button, one can access a literal world of information. Curiously, after thinking about my admission, I wondered about our result-oriented society and the longing for success. Hence, I typed "three easy steps" into the google search engine, figuring someone out there, regardless of their endeavor, wants success and a simple path to get there.

There were 417 million results for "three easy steps." People do resonate with this sentiment. I must admit, I like to keep things simple. Three easy steps to some kind of success? Sign me up.

The evangelistic endeavor is not a "three easy step" engagement. Rather, it is a step of faith.

We've noted some of the challenging consequences of sharing the gospel, including the not so desirable ones as seen in the efforts of our first century brethren. But be encouraged. The Bible is very clear, in principle, that the more seed one sows, the more fruit appears. And because Jesus promised to build His church through the testimony of His people, we can be of good cheer.

As a point of encouragement, note the example of the Apostle Paul, as he's used as a minister of reconciliation that leads to salvation. In Acts 16, Paul begins his second missionary journey, accompanied by Silas and Timothy. Their travels take them to Philippi, where we find them ministering one Sabbath day:

> Therefore, sailing from Troas, we ran a straight course to Samothrace, and the next day came to Neapolis, and from there to Philippi, which is the foremost city of that part of Macedonia, a colony. And we were staying in that city for some days. And on the Sabbath day we went out of the city to the riverside, where prayer was customarily made; and we sat down and spoke to the women who met there (Acts 16:11-13).

The Apostle Paul would often teach the things of the Kingdom in the synagogue during the Sabbath (see Acts 13:13-47) and more specifically—the good news of Jesus the Messiah. But here we find him at a rivers edge, teaching women. Apparently, there was no synagogue in Philippi, a leading city of the Roman province of Macedonia. In fact, the Jewish population must have been very small, as it only took ten Jewish men to complete the minyan or quorum. With no synagogue, worshippers met at the river, Paul addressed women, including Lydia, a gentile convert. This is what we might call, in hindsight, a divine appointment. Divine appointments often occur through prayer. And when our obedience meets God's providence, divine appointments happen.

Evangelism should begin on our knees. I have a pastor friend who told me he starts every day praying specifically for God to open doors, provide ministry opportunities, and orchestrate divine appointments. This certainly applies in the evangelistic endeavor.

In Colossians 4:2 Paul asked the church in Colosse to pray that "God would open to us a door for the word, to speak the mystery of Christ."

As the Lord directs the steps of His ambassadors (2 Corinthians 5:20), He also opens the hearts of people who hear the gospel. He does this through the power of the Holy Spirit, yet with whom He does this is quite a mystery.

We can't understand the true condition of the human heart, but the Lord can (Jeremiah 20:12, Luke 16:15, John 2:25, Acts 15:8). So how people may or may not respond to the gospel is ultimately an issue between them and the Lord. We plant, we sow, and we water in faith, but it is the Lord who gives the increase when there is an increase. As we've noted earlier, the human heart is likened to the soil in the parable of the soils (Matthew 13:1-9, 18-23). So we need to pray God would soften the hearts of people (make their hearts "good soil') to hear the gospel and receive the Lord.

God not only opens up the heart of Lydia, but her entire household:

Now a certain woman named Lydia heard us. She was a seller of purple from the city of Thyatira, who worshiped God. The Lord opened her heart to heed the things spoken by Paul. And when she and her household were baptized, she begged us, saying, "If you have judged me to be faithful to the Lord, come to my house and stay." So she persuaded us (Acts 16:14-15).

Lydia was a worshipper of God in the Old Testament sense. She hadn't heard of God's grace through the death and resurrection of Jesus. But the Lord opened her heart to respond to the things of God. Do you suppose Paul and Silas had prayed for open doors, open hearts, and divine appointments? Yes, and we see the Lord answering their prayer in opening her heart.

Yes, we are to pray for others: those we know, and those we have not yet met but are going to meet in His providence. We are to lovingly serve people. We are to proclaim the gospel as God opens doors for us to do so. But we can't open the human heart to the things of God. This is His work (John 6:44-45). So stop trying to "get them to see the light" based upon your own human effort and argumentation. Rather, pray God works in their heart and delivers them out of darkness and into the light (Colossians 1:13).

Seek to be faithful—faithful to plant, sow, and water through prayer, service, and proclamation—all done in love. And along the way praying that God will do what only He can do: give the increase.

Being About The Father's Business

When Jesus was just a boy of twelve years, He was separated from His family while in Jerusalem for Passover. His relieved parents found Him in the Temple, talking with the religious leaders. Upon finding Him, Mary said to Jesus, "Why have you done this to us? Look, Your father and I have sought You anxiously." Jesus responded in Luke 2:49, "Why did you seek Me? Did you not know that I must be about My Father's business?"

Jesus had a game plan: to be about the Father's business. As His servants, we have been given a game plan: "For we are His workmanship, created in Christ Jesus for good works, which God prepared beforehand that we should walk in them" (Ephesians 2:10).

C.S. Lewis felt this way about the Father's business. "The glory of God, and, as our only means of glorifying Him, the salvation of souls, is the real business of life." [39]

In personal evangelism, our agenda is to follow Jesus, be His witnesses in word and deed, and point people to Him. Jesus said, "Follow me and I will make you fishers of men" (Matthew 4:18-20). He also says, "Go and make disciples of all nations ... and I will be with you always" (Matthew 28:19-20). He reiterated the agenda in Acts 1:8, "But you shall receive power when the Holy Spirit has come upon you; and you shall be witnesses to Me in Jerusalem, and in all Judea and Samaria, and to the end of the earth." Jesus' agenda was to be about the Father's business and that should be our agenda.

So my brothers and sisters, be about the Father's business, sowing and watering, trusting God to give the increase in His good time.

Chapter 9

Interruption And Opportunity

Those larger than life balloons of our favorite television characters meandering down Fifth Avenue are awesome. The marching bands. The floats. The spectacle. The fun. New York City on the fourth Thursday in November. You guessed it: The Macy's Day Thanksgiving Parade in all its glory. Except of course, if the weather is horrid.

Living in the Big Apple for a number of years as a missionary gave me first hand access to the parade. Each Thanksgiving Day our ministry would hand out thousands of gospel tracts to revelers along the streets of the parade route. When the weather was mild and dry, it was quite fun, as folks are generally in a festive mood. And in my six years in New York, pleasant weather was generally the case. But not that year.

That year I was leading our outreach, inclement weather set in. It was a cold, wet, late November morning in the city that never sleeps. Awakening to raw weather on this particular morning, part of me wished I didn't have to get out of bed.

I rose before daybreak (note: not sunrise, as I never saw the sun that day). I had to make some decisions. Living in New York City means having contingency plans, especially when doing street evangelism. You know—blessed are the flexible, for they shall not be bent out of shape. On that chilly, rainy and windy morning, outdoor activity would need to be a last resort, and I chose to deploy much of our ministry team underground. The few that could be above ground on the street would have to hand out literature under awnings.

If you're not familiar with New York, then this may seem counterintuitive. Why do outreach underground for a parade that is on the street. Well, know that New York's subway system is always active, and many parade goers utilize the train to get into Manhattan, where the parade is located.

Seeking to make lemonade from a lemon of a weather day, our ministry team handed out over 10,000 gospel tracts and had a number of spiritual conversations with people.

One of the exciting dynamics of having much of the team deployed in subway holes, as they're commonly called, was that we would have an opportunity to interact with people we may not have otherwise met had we all been on the street. In fact, you might say this was a case of the weather creating not an interruption, but an opportunity.

We had a number of volunteers from area churches who served with our ministry that day, and no matter where I deployed them, they sought to shine the light of Christ.

The Lord can use people anywhere, and this was one such case where the rain outside led to contingency plans underground. As the saying goes, sometimes there is Plan A, Plan B, and Plan G—God's plan. Plan G on this day played out just fine, as interruption in the physical turned out to be an opportunity in the spiritual. There were people who took gospel literature underground that may have never even come across one of our ministers above ground. And so gospel seeds were planted and we praised God for all we were able to sow.

Life is filled with interruptions. And sometimes we can make no sense out of those unpleasant moments, events, or even seasons. But having confidence in God, we trust that He has plans and purposes that may not be in line with our own. Author Henry Blackaby wrote: "God has a right to interrupt your life. He is Lord. When you surrendered to Him, you acknowledged His right to help Himself to your life at his prerogative." [40] As the writer of Proverbs noted: "A man's heart plans his way, but the Lord directs his step" (Proverbs 16:9).

There is much to learn from studying the Apostle Paul's efforts to expand the Kingdom of God, and hopefully, much we can apply to our own lives as we seek to be change agents for Christ in the here and now.

As we explore a season of Paul's life from the book of Acts, a couple of principles stand out: first, we have much less control than we think—be okay with that; second, God is in total control—be okay with that.

Control is in the sovereign hand of almighty God. He is managing the events of man. History is "His Story."

Therefore, interruptions that may appear to be inconveniences in the natural may be opportunities in the spiritual. How so? Well, the Lord has a singular ability to place us in the right place at the right time in order to be witnesses for Him.

Case in point: the Apostle Paul's journey to Rome in Acts 27 and 28.

An Unexpected Journey

Following Paul's testimony before Festus and Agrippa in Caesarea in Acts 26, the apostle was placed with other prisoners on a boat and began a journey to Rome, where he was to face Caesar:

> "And when it was decided that we should sail to Italy, they delivered Paul and some other prisoners to one named Julius, a centurion of the Augustan Regiment. So, entering a ship of Adramyttium, we put to sea, meaning to sail along the coasts of Asia. Aristarchus, a Macedonian of Thessalonica, was with us. And the next day we landed at Sidon. And Julius treated Paul kindly and gave him liberty to go to his friends and receive care. When we had put to sea from there, we sailed under the shelter of Cyprus, because the winds were contrary. And when we had sailed over the sea which is off Cilicia and Pamphylia, we came to Myra, a city of Lycia. There the centurion found an Alexandrian ship sailing to Italy, and he put us on board" (Acts 27:1-6).

In the remainder of Acts 27, things get very interesting. Soon after setting sail from Myra, the weather began wreaking havoc, putting the boat and men on the boat in peril, and making them despair of all hope:

> "And running under the shelter of an island called Clauda, we secured the skiff with difficulty. When they had taken it on board, they used cables to undergird the ship; and fearing lest they should run aground on the Syrtis Sands, they struck sail and so were driven. And because we were exceedingly tempest-tossed, the next day they lightened the ship. On the third day we threw the ship's tackle overboard with our own hands. Now when neither sun nor stars appeared for many days, and no small tempest beat on us, all hope that we would be saved was finally given up" (Acts 27:16-20).

The captain ignored Paul's warning of impending doom, and continued to sail on. The weather worsened to the point of the men losing all hope of being saved. Amidst the tumult, Paul witnessed to the men and assures them they'll all live. Then they are spared when the boat shipwrecks at the island of Malta and the men make it to land, confirming Paul's words:

> When it was day, they did not recognize the land; but they observed a bay with a beach, onto which they planned to run the ship if possible. And they let go the anchors and left them in the sea, meanwhile loosing the rudder ropes; and they hoisted the mainsail to the wind and made for shore. But striking a place where two seas met, they ran the ship aground; and the prow stuck fast and remained immovable, but the stern was being broken up by the violence of the waves.

> And the soldiers' plan was to kill the prisoners, lest any of them should swim away and escape. But the centurion, wanting to save Paul, kept them from their purpose, and commanded that those who could swim should jump overboard first and get to land, and the rest, some on boards and some on parts of the ship. And so it was that they all escaped safely to land (Acts 27:39-46).

The tempest was not an interruption, but an opportunity for Paul. He spent the next three months ministering the gospel in Malta, all because of an "unforeseen" storm. To grasp the impact of their ministry, Luke records these words upon their leaving for Rome:

> Now when they had escaped, they then found out that the island was called Malta. And the natives showed us unusual kindness; for they kindled a fire and made us all welcome, because of the rain that was falling and because of the cold. But when Paul had gathered a bundle of sticks and laid them on the fire, a viper came out because of the heat, and fastened on his hand. So when the natives saw the creature hanging from his hand, they said to one another, "No doubt this man is a murderer, whom, though he has escaped the sea, yet justice does not allow to live." But he shook off the creature into the fire and suffered no harm. However, they were expecting that he would swell up or suddenly fall down dead.
>
> But after they had looked for a long time and saw no harm come to him, they changed their minds and said that he was a god. In that region there was an estate of the leading citizen of the island, whose name was Publius, who received us and entertained us courteously for three days. And it happened that the father of Publius lay sick of a fever and dysentery. Paul went in to him and prayed, and he laid his hands on him and healed him. So when this was done, the rest of those on the island who had diseases also came and were healed. They also honored us in many ways; and when we departed, they provided such things as were necessary (Acts 28:1–10).

To be sure, the honor and glory would ultimately be given to the Lord Jesus, the one who "causes all things to work together for good to those who love God, to those who are called according to His purpose" (Romans 8:28).

How do we respond to interruptions? No doubt, some of us deal with them better than others. When we look through the eyes of faith, sometimes those so-called interruptions may be opportunities in disguise.

Once, while walking out of the post office in our hometown of 4000 people in Jonesborough, TN, a middle-aged man looked at me. Wearing a backpack and holding a cane, he asked me for some money so he could get something to eat.

Since I had no cash, I told him I would buy him a sandwich if he wanted. He said that would be nice. During our drive to Subway, Brian shared his story of being homeless for the first time in his life. I asked him about his spiritual condition. He said he was a believer. I prayed for him in the car, bought him a meal and gave him a Bible. He was encouraged, and so was I.

I'm reluctant to tell that story, because other times in facing that same kind of situation, I'm frankly "too busy" to deal with it, and simply walk or drive past.

As we follow the Lord, we must be flexible enough to know that there is a plan A and sometimes a plan B, but most certainly there is always a Plan G—God's plan. Because "the mind of man plans his way, but the Lord directs his steps" (Proverbs 16:9).

"For we are His workmanship, created in Christ Jesus for good works, which God prepared beforehand so that we would walk in them" (Ephesians 2:10).

Sometimes opportunities to be witnesses for Jesus in word and deed are veiled in apparent interruptions. Therefore, do we love God enough to allow him to interrupt us? May we acknowledge this potential reality, committing our way to the Lord, asking Him to give us wisdom and discernment in such matters, for His Glory and for our testimony to others.

Bloom Where You're Planted

Just like Esther in the Old Testament, the Lord has strategically placed believers in a unique place at a unique time in order to fulfill His plans and purposes. To see this, we need eyes of faith. Sometimes we do see, yet there are other times we don't see the plan at all. In either case, we are always called to walk by faith.

And by the way, wherever you find yourself today as you read these words and think about your place and purpose, please remember that God has a plan for you. He's planted you "for such a time as this" (Esther 4:14).

Sometimes, we are grateful for where God has planted us, but there are times when we are not where *we* want to be. In other words, we may be planted in a locale, job situation, or life circumstance that is not what we would choose. The planting of God may be a moment in time, or a season of life. Perhaps you find yourself in that situation today. If not, just wait. Soon enough you will be.

It was July 2008. A missionary friend of mine named Susan and I were handing out gospel literature at an outdoor concert in a Long Island (NY) park—a place where the ministry we served with had experienced first amendment issues in the past. We were illegally detained and Susan willingly was arrested for trespassing. We could go to court. While being held by the authorities, we had a chance to witness to law enforcement officials and give testimony about Jesus. Later, in a court of law, our ministries' First Amendment right to distribute literature in that park was upheld.

As Paul and Silas were engaged in ministry, we examined a fascinating occurrence where they bloomed where they were planted. In this case, they were planted behind the bars of a prison cell.

After delivering a fortune-telling slave girl from a spirit of divination, her masters create a riot which results in Paul and Silas being thrown in jail (Acts 16:16-24).

While there, the two prayed and sang hymns of praise. Other prisoners listened to them (Acts 16:25). And not just the prisoners, but the prison guard also listened:

> Suddenly there was a great earthquake, so that the foundations of the prison were shaken; and immediately all the doors were opened and everyone's chains were loosed. And the keeper of the prison, awaking from sleep and seeing the prison doors open, supposing the prisoners had fled, drew his sword and was about to kill himself. But Paul called with a loud voice, saying, "Do yourself no harm, for we are all here." Then he

called for a light, ran in, and fell down trembling before Paul and Silas. And he brought them out and said, *"Sirs, what must I do to be saved?"* (Acts 16:26-30, italics mine).

I find it remarkable that seeing the prison doors open, the prisoners didn't run for it. Now, we don't know what Paul and Silas may have shared with the prisoners, but obviously, there was a powerful influence upon them.

Upon hearing the word of the Lord, the jailer and his entire household were baptized:

> And they said, "Believe in the Lord Jesus, and you will be saved, you and your household." and they spoke the word of the Lord to him and to all who were in his house. And he took them the same hour of the night and washed their wounds; and he was baptized at once, he and all his family. Then he brought them up into his house and set food before them. And he rejoiced along with his entire household that he had believed in God. (Acts 16:31-34)

What happens next is confounding:

> And when it was day, the magistrates sent the officers, saying, "Let those men go."
>
> So the keeper of the prison reported these words to Paul, saying, "The magistrates have sent to let you go. Now therefore depart, and go in peace" (Acts 16:35-36).

What? Let them go? We don't know about the other prisoners, but Paul and Silas willingly stayed in the jail overnight—at least whatever was left of it.

Paul and Silas had been jailed illegally. They were Roman citizens. And now they were being released and exhorted to leave the city:

> But Paul said to them, "They have beaten us publicly, uncondemned, men who are Roman citizens, and have thrown us into prison; and do they now throw us out secretly? No. Let them come themselves and take us out." The police reported

these words to the magistrates, and they were afraid when they heard that they were Roman citizens. So they came and apologized to them. And they took them out and asked them to leave the city" (Acts 16:37-39 ESV).

You could say, that in one sense, the sovereign hand of God was orchestrating all these tumultuous events for the jailer and his household to be saved. And I even wonder about the prisoners. God planted Paul and Silas in a jail so they could bloom—be a witness for Jesus.

Now when Susan and I were detained illegally in 2008, it would be great to tell you God worked miraculous signs and wonders and people were saved. That was not the case.

But I can tell you there was great comfort knowing God had a plan in the planting—for we certainly were given an opportunity to be a distinct witness for Jesus.

God has a plan in the planting of your life. It may be in a moment of time, or a season of life. For "there is a time and purpose for every season under heaven" (Ecclesiastes 3:1, *my paraphrase*). What is that plan, you wonder? To bloom, of course. The blooming being a distinct witness for Jesus in your unique sphere of influence.

Where you live, work, shop, go to school, travel; wherever God has you planted you at any particular moment or season of life, you have a grand opportunity—an opportunity to bloom. And while it can be in the midst of need as we've highlighted, it can also be in the midst of plenty. So, regardless of whether the planting be a moment or season that is uncomfortable, desirable, or otherwise in our estimation, take advantage of the opportunity to bloom for Jesus.

Lord, thank You for planting me where You have chosen. May I bloom for Your glory. Amen.

Chapter 10

Mighty In The Scriptures

It's not a pleasant memory, but one I will recall, in hopes of redeeming that time for our purpose. I was a junior in high school and taking a trigonometry class. One of our exercises involved calculating airplane navigation.

Now as much as I enjoy air travel, it pained me to plot vectors on graphs with a pencil, a ruler, and protractor. Additionally, we had to factor in wind speed, ground speed, plane speed, beginning points, ending points, and other variables into the various formulas. Imagine the frustration of getting one computation wrong, or in my case getting many of them wrong. Confused yet? I was. With math, confusion came to me naturally. As I struggled in dealing with the various factors to consider, part of me cried out, "What is the point?"

But, as my teacher pointed out, while this may have seemed like some kind of abstract exercise to students, on an airfield it's absolutely essential for the pilot to get the flight plan right. Traveling long distances at high speeds requires precise study and planning. Who knew getting from point A to B would require such acuity?

Understanding and incorporating wind conditions is one component critical to the flight plan. An aircraft's speed can be greatly enhanced or diminished by the wind. This is the reason for the consideration of two speeds: ground speed and air speed. Ground speed is the speed at which an aircraft is moving with respect to the ground. Air speed is the speed of an aircraft in relation to the surrounding air. Wind speed is the physical speed of the air relative to the ground. Air speed, ground speed and wind speed are all vector quantities.

I did take some solace in knowing that if I had computed the right numbers, the formula would provide the correct answer. For example, the flight time is the actual time an aircraft is in the air flying from its departure point to its destination point. The computed flight time (when the speed is assumed to be constant) is given by the equation: Time = Distance divided by Speed. Simple, right? Not for me.

We've taken note of the growing opposition to the Christian faith. We've used the image of gale force winds blowing against our efforts to spread the gospel. In a sense, we've been looking at all the elements necessary to calculate a way to become a faithful witness in a rapidly changing culture.

So far so good, but we must look at another important factor in our calculations: the handling of Scripture.

Just as a pilot must be prepared to deal with various flying conditions, we also need to be prepared to deal with whatever spiritual conditions we find ourselves in. In our Christian walk, stewardship of God's Word will define much of who we are and will affect the impact of our Christian testimony. "All Scripture," Paul said, "is God-breathed and is useful for teaching, rebuking, correcting and training in righteousness, so that the man of God may be thoroughly equipped for every good work" (2 Timothy 3:16-17).

Additionally, when we seek the Lord in His Word, we are not simply engaging His truth, we're engaging Him. As author Henry Blackaby states: "Scripture is not a concept; scripture is a person (John 1:1,14). When you stand before the Word of God, you are not merely encountering a concept; you are standing face-to-face with God." [41]

We broach the topic of the stewardship of God's Word not only because it's important in our time, but because it's a transcendent foundational topic for every generation of the church. Often in our Christian life we learn of stewarding our money, time, and bodies. Here we want to talk about being a good steward of God's Word itself.

Part of my desire for this project is to inspire believers in America to delve into the book of Acts specifically, but to get into the Bible in general. I believe, for many reasons, that our understanding, internalizing, and application of God's Word is key to walking with the Lord into the gale of our time.

My best friend Daryl, who graduated to heaven a few years ago, used to say things like: "Larry, if you're not getting into the Word of God, what are you getting into?" and, "Get into the Word of God and let the Word of God get into you, because if you don't, you'll get into the world and the world will get into you."

Many books have been written on Bible study. My purpose is not to add to their number, but to focus on the study of Acts and what it can teach us about being faithful witnesses in contemporary America.

A Starting Point

Before we examine Apollos, one of our first century brethren who is described as a "man mighty in the Scriptures," we begin with a few foundational verses and even a whole chapter highlighting the importance of God's Word in our life:

Matthew 4:4 (see also Deuteronomy 8:3). "Man shall not live by bread alone, but by every word that proceeds from the mouth of God."

John 17:17. "Thy Word is truth."

Psalm 119:1-4. The longest of psalms and chapters in the Bible, Psalm 119, with its 176 verses, touches on various themes associated with understanding, obeying, and applying God's Word. Here are the first 4 verses of this rich Psalm:

> "Blessed are the undefiled in the way, who walk in the law of the Lord. Blessed are those who keep His testimonies, who seek Him with the whole heart. They also do no iniquity; They walk in His ways. You have commanded us to keep Your precepts diligently."

2 Timothy 2:15. "Be diligent to present yourself approved to God, a worker who does not need to be ashamed, rightly dividing the word of truth."

Hebrews 4:12-13. "For the word of God is living and powerful, and sharper than any two-edged sword, piercing even to the division of soul and spirit, and of joints and marrow, and is a discerner of the thoughts and intents of the heart. And there is no creature hidden from His sight, but all things are naked and open to the eyes of Him to whom we must give account."

Psalm 19:7-13. "The law of the Lord is perfect, converting the soul; The testimony of the Lord is sure, making wise the simple; The statutes of the Lord are right, rejoicing the heart; The commandment of the Lord is pure, enlightening the eyes; The fear of the Lord is clean, enduring forever; The judgments of the Lord are true and righteous altogether. More to be desired are they than gold, Yea, than much fine gold; Sweeter also than honey and the honeycomb. Moreover by them Your servant is warned, and in keeping them there is great reward."

And we could go on. But this provides but a taste of the riches of His words about His Word.

Countering The Gale—Our Offensive Weapon

Whether we were living in America under the bubble of our Judeo-Christian heritage, in the "doldrums," or in our current cultural climate where the tempest rages, spiritual warfare is constant. It may take different forms and manifest in different ways, but make no mistake—there has been, and will continue to be, spiritual opposition blowing against the agenda of the church as it seeks to fulfill the Great Commission.

In Ephesians 6, the Apostle Paul describes the spiritual war that the devil and his minions wage against us. In verses 10-18, Paul describes the whole armor of God we are to put on in this fight. In verse 17, he notes the only offensive component of the armor: the "Sword of the Spirit," the Word of God.

Paul added in 2 Corinthians 10:3-5:

> For though we walk in the flesh, we do not war according to the flesh. For the weapons of our warfare are not carnal but

mighty in God for pulling down strongholds, casting down arguments and every high thing that exalts itself against the knowledge of God.

The truth of God's word is a powerful weapon. Jesus said in John 8:32, "You shall know the truth and the truth shall set you free."

Use the weapon of the truth to confront error, to blunt the attack against truth, and to walk in the freedom which Christ has provided. With the Word of God in our minds and hearts, we can walk into the gale.

Apollos—A First Century Example

Billy Graham once was asked, "Billy, how do you grow in the Christian life?" Billy responded, "That's simple. If you want to grow in the Christian life, wallow in God's Word like a pig wallows in the mud."

Sometimes the most basic of endeavors are also the most profound and powerful.

Understanding and application of God's Word is essential to living the Christian life, in any and all times.

In one sense, if we want to become mighty in the Scriptures, we need to wallow in the Scriptures. In Acts 18, we are introduced to Apollos, a man "mighty in the Scriptures" who undoubtedly spent much time in the Word. His knowledge and use of God's word in his witness for Jesus is an excellent example for us:

> "Now a certain Jew named Apollos, born at Alexandria, an eloquent man and mighty in the Scriptures, came to Ephesus. This man had been instructed in the way of the Lord; and being fervent in spirit, he spoke and taught accurately the things of the Lord, though he knew only the baptism of John" (Acts 18:24-25).

Apollos came from Alexandria, Egypt—one of the best learning centers in the ancient world. "The Scriptures" to him would have been the Old Testament, the Bible to Jewish people in the first century. All of the New Testament letters had not yet been written and compiled into the New Testament canon.

Being mighty in the Scriptures is not only having head knowledge of the truth, but also applying that knowledge to daily life and ministry. Apollos not only was "instructed in the way of the Lord," he was "teaching accurately the things of the Lord."

Another aspect of being mighty in the Scriptures bears mentioning: application of God's Word. In Ezra, Apollos would have had a tremendous biblical example that would have shaped his own life and ministry. Ezra 10:10 states: "For Ezra had prepared his heart to seek the Law of the Lord, and to do it, and to teach statutes and ordinances in Israel."

Ezra gave us a pattern we can follow today:

Ezra's heart sought the Lord in His Word, the Law;

He applied God's Word;

He taught it.

The point for us is this: before we can *apply* God's Word in our lives, we must first *know* God's Word. And knowing takes work. We must regularly take in the Word, so we can be spiritually nourished and energized to do God's will.

As we noted above, (it bears repeating) Jesus' said in Matthew 4:4, "Man shall not live by bread alone, but by every word that proceeds from the mouth of God" (see also Deuteronomy 8:3).

But feeding on God's Word is one thing. We also need to apply it. This is essential in being mighty in the Scriptures. As James 1:25 states: "But he who looks into the perfect law of liberty and continues in it, and is not a forgetful hearer but a doer of the work, this one will be blessed in what he does."

Growing In God's Word Requires Humility

Although Apollos spoke and taught accurately the things of the Lord, his understanding was limited. He had the Old Testament and the teaching of John the Baptist: "...he spoke and taught accurately the things of the Lord, though he knew only the baptism of John" (Acts

18:24-25).

And what was John's understanding?

In Luke 3:3 we are told: "He (John the Baptist) went into all the country around the Jordan preaching the baptism of repentance for the forgiveness of sins." John identified Jesus as the Messiah and Son of God. In John 1:29, he said of Jesus: "Look, the Lamb of God, who takes away the sin of the world." (see also Isaiah 53:4-7), and then added: "I have seen and I testify that this is the Son of God" (John 1:34).

In short, Apollos, in the tradition of John the Baptist, was teaching that the way of forgiveness was through repentance of sin and baptism.

Now Apollos was teaching accurately the way of Jesus as best he knew, yet his teaching was incomplete. He didn't fully understand the significance of Christ's death and resurrection, nor would he have been acquainted with the coming of the Holy Spirit and birth of the church at Pentecost. So, here we see another exemplary quality in the man—his humility:

"So he began to speak boldly in the synagogue. When Priscilla and Aquila heard him, they took him aside and *explained to him the way of God more accurately*" (Acts 18:26, italics mine).

Paul had met Aquila and Priscilla earlier in Acts 18:2-3. They probably were believers when they met Paul, but if not, they became believers while spending time with him. Consequently, they understood the grace of God found in the gospel message—believing in the death and resurrection of Jesus.

If Apollos preached in the tradition of John the Baptist he would place insufficient emphasis on the grace of God. Hence, his teaching would not have made it clear that: Forgiveness of sins was through faith in the sacrifice Jesus made at Calvary. Repentance must be accompanied by a willingness to follow Jesus, trusting fully in his saving work on the cross.

That Apollos, a mighty preacher and scholar, would consent to being instructed by a lowly tentmaker and his wife attests to his humility.

No matter how learned we are in God's Word, nobody ever arrives. We are always in the process of learning more. The Psalmist wrote, "He guides the humble in what is right and teaches them his way" (Psalm 25:4). Growing requires humility, for humility and teachability go hand in hand. Apollos learned "the way of God more accurately," demonstrating humility. And when we humble ourselves in the sight of the Lord, "he will lift us up" (James 4:10).

Fishers Of Men

After receiving instruction from Aquila and Priscilla, Apollos went on to disciple believers and be a witness to unbelievers with a fuller understanding of God's grace found in Jesus and the gospel message:

> And when he desired to cross to Achaia, the brethren wrote, exhorting the disciples to receive him; and when he arrived, he greatly helped those who had believed through grace; for he vigorously refuted the Jews publicly, showing from the Scriptures that Jesus is the Christ (Acts 18:27-28).

To strive to become mighty in the Scriptures is no doubt a godly aspiration. Yet, as with any discipline, it takes time and commitment. Apollos could effectively use the Scriptures because he had spent much time in the Scriptures. For us, time and commitment invested in growing in God's Word is going to be opposed by the enemy of our souls—the devil and his minions (Ephesians 6:10-18, 1 Peter 5:8) and our old man, the flesh (Romans 7:13-25, Galatians 5:16-25).

Apollos was fulfilling his role in the Great Commission, utilizing his gift of teaching to strengthen the church and witness to the lost. And what about you? Do you know what your spiritual gifts are and how He wants you to utilize them for His glory?

We are called to be not only hearers of the Word, but also doers of the Word (James 1:22-25). So becoming mighty in the Scriptures includes both understanding and application of God's Word. What does this mean for your walk with God in the here and now amid this culture? Jesus calling the first disciples is instructive:

> And Jesus, walking by the Sea of Galilee, saw two brothers, Simon called Peter, and Andrew his brother, casting a net into the sea; for they were fishermen. Then He said to them, "Follow Me, and I will make you fishers of men." They immediately left their nets and followed Him (Matthew 4:18-20).

What does it mean to be a "fisher of men?"

When Peter and Andrew heard those words from Jesus, I wonder what thoughts ran through their mind. "Fishers of men? Really? What's Jesus talking about?"

In one sense, it was all about reorientation. They knew about fishing for fish. But fishing for men? I suppose Jesus' words, as they often did in the gospels, initially confuse and confound them.

Specifically, the Lord would redeem, shape, and utilize their experience as fisherman to now function in a new paradigm—the Kingdom of God. Ultimately, in time, they would come to understand their Kingdom responsibility as "fishers of men."

Jesus, in calling them to follow Him, could have used any phrase. I find it striking that His calling regarding their future Kingdom endeavors included their past earthly experience.

And therein lies a powerful application for you and me.

I've played tennis most of my life, including working fourteen years as a professional tennis coach. And I can tell you God has used my tennis experiences in my witness for Jesus Christ. In fact, I've written a book on personal evangelism entitled *Serving In His Court: Biblical Principles For Personal Evangelism From The Heart Of A Coach* that utilizes the motif of tennis in equipping believers to fulfill the Great Commission.

Jesus made Peter and Andrew fishers of men. He's used my tennis experience in developing my witness for Him. How about you?

God can and does use our past to glorify His name in the present. Whatever gifts, abilities, and experiences He has endowed you with,

He can and will use them to shape you into the witness He desires you to be. The key is to simply follow Him, as Peter and Andrew did so long ago.

So follow Jesus and commit your way to Him, allowing Him to use the gifts, abilities, and experiences He's given you, for people and ultimately for His Glory.

Bible Study Resources And Methods

In our cyber-driven information age, we have the privilege of having access to incredible Bible study tools, all with a touch of a keypad. If you're more traditional, print materials may be more your speed. In any case, utilizing Bible commentaries, concordances, dictionaries, lexicons, biblical maps and encyclopedias—via print or online—will enhance your understanding of God's Word and help you better understand Him and His will.

Additionally, there are a variety of methods to employ when opening God's Word. Those methods include topical studies, character study, word studies, and inductive Bible study. Whatever method you use, and you may use any and all, be regular and systematic. Again, solid internet resources are myriad and can benefit your journey.

Ultimately, whatever methods and resources you utilize, get into the Word of God and let the Word of God get into you. Remember the illustration from a few pages earlier? Billy Graham was asked, "Billy, how do you grow in the Christian life?" He replied, "That's simple. If you want to grow in the Christian life, wallow in God's Word like a pig wallows in the mud."

Simple. Powerful. Yet challenging.

Stay Focused—A Twenty-First Century Exhortation

We live in curious times. While our present day has been called the Age of Information, it may also be called the Age of Distraction.

Life today is filled with distraction. Between our business, our gadgets, our entertainment, and the overall demands and enticements of our day, and the chaos and pandemonium of current events, we can become overwhelmed by it all—so much so that we forget what life is all about.

Even as I pen these words on the computer, I need to stay disciplined to avoid email, Facebook, and the internet—all available at a click of a button.

Distraction affects many areas of our lives, including the area of our witness. In fact, distraction may be a powerful tool in the hands of the enemy in keeping us from focusing time on the Lord—in His Word and in prayer—and from focusing our energy on sharing the love of God in word and deed.

Henry David Thoreau, is well-known for his book *Walden*, a reflection upon simple living in natural surroundings. In this seminal work he stated: "Our life is frittered away by detail ... simplify, simplify." [42] And this coming from a man who lived in the nineteenth century.

One can only imagine Thoreau's commentary upon our twenty-first century information explosion, technological toys, and cultural climate dominated by entertainment.

Distraction can cause us to lose sight of the main thing in life. And what is that main thing? Relationships. Jesus reminds us of this simple, yet profound, relational priority:

> "'You shall love the Lord your God with all your heart, with all your soul, and with all your mind.' This is the first and great commandment. And the second is like it: 'You shall love your neighbor as yourself'" (Matthew 22:37-39).

When we love God and others, we're moving in the right direction, for our spiritual flight plan helps us accurately navigate the winds blowing against us. Becoming mighty in the Scriptures is not only about what's in our head's, but what flows out of our hearts.

When a pilot meticulously makes a flight plan, he does so for a purpose: to get the plane from point A to point B. In similar fashion, when we spend time with the Lord and seek to become mighty in the

Scriptures, "rightly dividing the Word of truth," (2 Timothy 2:15) it's also for a purpose: to love God and others. Our theology must become biology and when it does, we are not only hearing, learning, and growing in God's Word, we are *doing* God's Word. People are blessed, God is glorified, and we are satisfied in Him. Amen.

Chapter 11

Trial And Testimony

Deadliest Catch is a documentary television series that follows real life events on the vast Bering Sea aboard various crab fishing boats during two of the crab fishing seasons, the October king crab season and the January snow crab season. The Aleutian Islands port of Dutch Harbor, Alaska, is the base of operations for the fishing fleet.

When the show began in 2005, I was a big fan, faithfully watching the program for a few seasons. Between the personalities, the wonder of those huge crabs, and the challenge of staying alive on a boat during unpredictable and potentially dangerous ocean conditions, made the show, at least for me, must-see TV. And as of this writing, the show is still going strong.

The show's title, *Deadliest Catch,* comes from the inherent high risk of injury or death associated with the work. Alaskan crab fishing is one of the most dangerous jobs in the world. Additionally, the series also documents the dangers of being on a boat in the Bering Sea, amid some of the coldest and stormiest waters on earth. Being a captain of a fishing boat is challenging. But captaining a fishing boat in conditions like those featured on *Deadliest Catch,* takes the word "challenging" to a whole other level.

Captains need grace under pressure, because massive storms can erupt on the Bearing Sea without warning, putting the crew and any fishing activities in peril. Sometimes keeping the boat afloat can become an issue, if a storm's intensity rises enough. Add to the pressure of the job itself, which entails fishing and catching a haul of crab that will pay the bills and hopefully more during the off-fishing season, and you can imagine the captain's plight.

Can you say drama? Along with the drama and pressure of it all, these captains need to perform well amidst the intensity of the moment. In short, to be a captain in *Deadliest Catch*, one needs to be able to perform with grace under pressure.

As we think about our current cultural climate and the drama and storms facing the church in America, we are confronted with the reality that being a testimony may sometimes be incredibly difficult. For example, if you're a baker and have convictions leading to reservations about making a cake for a homosexual wedding—that's pressure. If you're in a position to stand up for the fact that there is a difference between boys and girls—the biology is clear—that is pressure.

Or how about facing opposition to the displaying the Ten Commandments, American flag or Nativity—that's pressure. And if someone wants you to remain silent about Jesus in any other situation, whatever that may be—that is pressure.

As I pen these words, our cultural climate is challenging and pressure-packed. For you and me, depending on where we are and the various situations we find ourselves, the degree of opposition is different, no doubt. But all of us are impacted in some way by the pressure of those who want our testimony silenced and our faith kept in the closet.

As we think about remaining true to our Christian convictions amidst the gales of opposition we face, we find an inspirational and instructional passage in the book of Acts. And the person we focus on who exemplifies grace under pressure is, again, none other than the Apostle Paul.

We can learn much about sharing our testimonies as we briefly explore how Paul provided his testimony while under intense pressure.

What's Your Story?

What's your story? It certainly is a topic that on occasion comes up in conversation, during an interview, and in other venues. For most of us, sharing some of our story is in the context of safe, non-threatening situations. But what of the rising pressure against believers sharing their faith worldwide, even here in the United States? When given an opportunity to stand up and speak for the truth amidst the pressure to shut up, how might you respond? How should you respond?

The Apostle Paul was often thrust into dangerous, emotion-filled, tumultuous moments where he gave witness under immense pressure. He is a tremendous example of grace under pressure amidst the swirl of chaos that can characterize gospel opposition.

I find it quite fascinating that Luke, under the inspiration of the Holy Spirit, includes Paul giving testimony on no less than four separate challenging occasions in Acts 22–26:

Acts 22: He addressed a Jewish mob in Jerusalem.

Acts 23: He addressed the Sanhedrin also in Jerusalem.

Acts 24: He gave a defense before Felix, Governor of Judea, in Caesarea.

Acts 25 and 26: He testified before King Agrippa, also in Caesarea.

There is much in these passages that we could discuss, and I encourage you to study those accounts more deeply than what we'll cover in this chapter, discovering more principles and personal applications on your own. For our purposes, I offer one principle to ponder from each of these four testimonies.

Contextualize Your Story (Acts 21:27-22:24)

The setting. Paul arrived in Jerusalem in Acts 21. By this time, his reputation had preceded him. Upon being recognized at the temple, an angry mob sought his harm (v. 27–31). After being taken from the mob and interrogated by the Roman commander, Paul was given permission to address the same mob that had murder on its mind—his murder (32–40).

In giving testimony of God's grace in his life, Paul provided his audience context:

> "I am indeed a Jew, born in Tarsus of Cilicia, but brought up in this city at the feet of Gamaliel, taught according to the strictness of our fathers' law, and was zealous toward God as you all are today. I persecuted this Way to the death, binding and delivering into prisons both men and women, as also the high priest bears me witness, and all the council of the elders, from whom I also received letters to the brethren, and went to Damascus to bring in chains even those who were there to Jerusalem to be punished" (Acts 22:3-6).

Once a murderer of those following Jesus, Paul now was willing to lay down his life for Jesus (Acts 21:13). This stark contrast of the ambitious Saul's conversion is powerful.

Paul established his Jewish pedigree and training to this Jewish audience, and in doing so, identified with them. In sharing his persecution of believers, he also connects with the mob, who was persecuting him. Paul was well-versed in reading and understanding people—Jew and Gentile alike. He knew power and political structures. He knew the weaknesses and vulnerabilities of his audiences and it made his gospel proclamation even more effective.

In this setting, Paul in essence is saying, "I know how you feel. I felt the same way." Soon enough he'll add in so many words, "But I found out Y'shua (Jesus) is Messiah and Lord" (Acts 22:6-21).

Everyone has a past. What is your BC (before Christ) experience? Communicate those elements and experiences that shaped your previous "God paradigm." This is important because everybody has a belief system, whether it be some form of atheism, agnosticism, or religion.

The context of where you came from will bring into sharp relief the difference the Lord has made in your life. The gospel is transformative, and that transformation is personal. Jesus stated, "I have come that they may have life, and that they may have it more abundantly" (John 10:10). Jesus changes everyone who comes to Him.

For example, when speaking with a Jewish person, I share from my Jewish background:

"I grew up in a reform Jewish household, a liberal Jewish religious expression. Our family was more culturally and socially Jewish than religiously and spiritually. Yet I received religious training, including becoming Bar Mitzvah (a ceremonial right of passage when a Jewish boy becomes a man) and always believed in God.

"When I came to believe in Jesus as Messiah and Lord in 1987, I was transformed."

In sharing with an individual or audience, I will sometimes state: "How is it possible that this Jewish man (speaking of myself), who for the first 23 years of his life, uttered the name of Jesus only in vain; now, for the last 30 (and counting) years, calls Him Messiah, Savior, Lord, and God?"

Transformation. The difference Jesus has made in our life is a difference we want to share. Before I came to faith, I walked in fear, without direction, and without hope. Now I experience abundant love, joy, and peace that transcends my circumstances, which frankly, at times, are quite painful.

And you? What shaped your God-paradigm growing up? How did you get here from there? Who were you before you trusted in Jesus and what difference has He made in your life? Providing context will authenticate and personalize your story.

What aspect of your audience's God-paradigm can you relate to and connect with? Listening and learning about them plays a critical role in facilitating your witness.

As you have faith-based conversations with people, remember, there is no-one-size-fits-all when attempting to connect with an individual. Ask the Lord to give you wisdom in this area and actively listen, so you can speak directly into their reality.

As the Lord provides opportunity to give testimony, whether in a friendly or hostile environment, be ready to contextualize your story and speak to your audience's reality for the glory of Jesus and benefit of your audience.

"A word fitly spoken is like apples of gold in settings of silver" (Proverbs 25:11).

Speak Into Your Audience's Reality (Acts 22:30-23:10)

The party crashers had arrived. It was the annual Israel Day Parade, along Fifth Avenue in Manhattan. Our team of missionaries were wearing shirts that stated in Hebrew and in English—"Jesus is Messiah." Over 100,000 people lined up along the parade route to cheer Jewish groups, floats and others making a statement in support of Israel.

As you might imagine, our group wasn't so well received.

I experienced real trepidation as we handed out gospel tracts and spoke with anyone open to conversing about Jesus. And God was faithful.

My most memorable encounter that day occurred along a path in Central Park, just adjacent to the parade route. I was cornered by two young Jewish men, who loudly interrogated me regarding my presence at the event. As I began sharing truth with them, they were none too pleased with any of my words. People along the path began to stop and see if a riot would break out.

I took advantage of the opportunity to share loud enough for all to hear. And thankfully, no physical harm was done to me. The young men soon left and the small crowd dispersed.

Incredibly, with one simple statement on a t-shirt—"Jesus is Messiah"—we created a powerful reaction. Among today's unbelieving Jews, virtually any kind of Jewish belief and expression is generally considered acceptable, except belief in Jesus. In fact, 2000 years of anti-Semitism, real and perceived, under the banner of Christianity, evokes visceral suspicion from the Jewish community toward Jesus followers.

In Acts 23 we find Paul in Jerusalem giving testimony before a very hostile group, the Sanhedrin. Here, the Apostle makes one statement that evoked a polarizing response and from it, we draw out this evangelistic principle to our contemporary witness.

The Setting. After addressing the mob, Paul was arrested by a Roman commander, then interrogated and scourged. Upon learning of his Roman citizenship, the commander released Paul and convened an unofficial meeting between Paul and the Jewish Sanhedrin. The Sanhedrin, made up of both Sadducees and Pharisees, was the supreme Jewish religious body at the time. Paul took advantage of this opportunity to share truth that compels a defense and creates a conflict:

> But when Paul perceived that one part were Sadducees and the other Pharisees, he cried out in the council, "Men and brethren, I am a Pharisee, the son of a Pharisee; concerning the hope and resurrection of the dead I am being judged." And when he had said this, a dissension arose between the Pharisees and the Sadducees; and the assembly was divided. For Sadducees say that there is no resurrection—and no angel or spirit; but the Pharisees confess both. Then there arose a loud outcry. And the scribes of the Pharisees' party arose and protested, saying, "We find no evil in this man; but if a spirit or an angel has spoken to him, let us not fight against God." Now when there arose a great dissension, the commander, fearing lest Paul might be pulled to pieces by them, commanded the soldiers to go down and take him by force from among them, and bring him into the barracks (Acts 23:6-10).

With one statement Paul rocked their world and brought down their "Paul-bashing" party. Here, the Apostle shaped his defense around the resurrection. Why? Because among the Sanhedrin, Paul "perceived that one part were Sadducees and the other Pharisees" (Acts 23:6). Paul, himself raised a Pharisee (Philippians 3:5), understood resurrection was a sharp point of contention between the two groups. In fact, the concept of resurrection was perhaps the biggest theological difference between the two groups. In light of this, Paul exclaimed, "Concerning the hope and resurrection of the dead I am being judged" (Acts 23:6).

This hot button issue was central both to the gospel message and to Paul's statement. I find it fascinating that the name of Jesus isn't mentioned. Yet the Sanhedrin certainly would have understood the claims of the early church regarding His resurrection.

The Pharisees sided with Paul. The Sadducees became incredulous. As the two sides argued, Paul was whisked away by a Roman commander.

It's also intriguing that the Scripture records the salvation of Pharisees (Acts 15:5), but not Sadducees.

As you interact with people in your own sphere of influence and have conversations about spiritual issues, be aware of your audience's reality and address that reality. In doing so, you affirm that person or people and provide the platform to connect on a personal level.

For example, in the summer of 2015, I spent a week barnstorming through Honduras doing ministry with an indigenous pastor friend name Louis. While addressing a high school in Honduras, I shared my testimony, mostly from my high school days. When speaking to a group of athletes, I'll draw from my tennis playing and coaching experience. And years ago while doing mission work in New York City, I ministered at Teen Challenge, a ministry for people struggling with life-controlling addictions, I shared much about my own drug-addiction struggles prior to salvation and how, through Christ, I now am clean.

Know and speak to your audience's reality. Doing so will make your witness personal and powerful.

Boldly And Directly Challenge Your Audience (Acts 23:23-24:27)

During my missionary life in New York City, I ministered to one Jewish man who was enthralled by and attracted to Jesus. He wanted to learn more about Jesus with me.

Taking a few visits to his apartment on the Upper East Side of Manhattan, I opened up the Gospel of John, sharing some of Jesus' claims to be the Jewish Messiah.

He seemed to be resonating with what the Bible was teaching, with one exception. Soon after arriving at his apartment for another Bible study, he stated in so many words, "You're making me very uncomfortable."

I said, "How so?"

He replied, "The Jesus you're presenting from the Bible is not the

Jesus I've been thinking about. I like a lot of things about Him, except for His claim to be the only way to God." He was referring to Jesus' words in John 14:6, "I am the way, the truth, and the life. No one comes to the Father except through Me."

I looked at him calmly and directly, "You know. Maybe that's exactly the way you're supposed to feel."

Conviction is powerful. Truth pierces "even to the division of soul and spirit" (Hebrews 4:12).

In conversation with people, there are appropriate times to set aside pleasantries and social graces for bold, direct, and sometimes challenging words. Regarding faith-based conversations, this time for bluntness requires wisdom, discernment and faith. There is no formula. It may be in an initial conversation or it may occur after a relationship has been established, a connection built upon time, rapport and trust.

In his third testimony in this section of Acts, we touch upon a fascinating encounter between Paul and Felix, Governor of Judea. Here we explore another witnessing principle that can inform our witness today:

The setting. Paul, having been accused of sedition against Rome, sacrilege and sectarianism by the Jewish religious authorities, was brought before Felix, Governor of Judea.

Following Paul's initial defense of himself, where he finally states that he is simply on trial for believing in "the resurrection of the dead" (Acts 24:21), Felix puts Paul under house arrest. This imprisonment lasts two years, during which time Paul would have opportunities to witness to the governor, including this interaction in Acts 24:24-25:

> And after some days, when Felix came with his wife Drusilla, who was Jewish, he sent for Paul and heard him concerning the faith in Christ. *Now as he reasoned about righteousness, self-control, and the judgment to come, Felix was afraid and answered, "Go away for now; when I have a convenient time I will call for you."* Meanwhile he also hoped that money would

be given him by Paul, that he might release him. Therefore he sent for him more often and conversed with him (italics mine).

As God opened up a door of opportunity to witness to Felix, Paul boldly, directly, and courageously challenged Felix with God's standard of righteousness and self-control. Drusilla, was someone else's wife when Felix lured her away to become his third wife. Obviously, lacking righteousness and self-control and facing the judgement to come, Felix is convicted. In fear, he sends Paul away. Conviction of sin will do one of two things: draw a person to the Lord or send them running. In this instance, Felix flees, sending Paul away.

When people are willing to interact over the gospel, it's okay to challenge them with truth. And let's be honest, the truth cuts (Hebrews 4:12-13). Certainly we should go to God on behalf of people before we go to people on behalf of God. In humility and gentleness, take opportunity to be direct, speaking the truth in love.

Paul would have future opportunities to share with Felix, although the governor's motives were mixed at best (Acts 24-26-27). And you can bet Paul took advantage of them!

As a postscript regarding my witness to the gentlemen in New York, that was the last time we visited. I was grateful for the opportunity to share the biblical Jesus. Part of the exclusivity of the gospel is that God requires us to come to Him on His terms (John 14:6), not ours. On the other hand, the grace of God's inclusivity is that He "so loved the world, that He sent His only begotten Son, that whosoever believes in Him should not perish but have everlasting life" (John 3:16).

As you engage in faith-based conversations with others, the appropriate time to boldly and directly challenge your audience requires wisdom and grace:

> Walk in wisdom toward those who are outside, redeeming the time. Let your speech always be with grace, seasoned with salt, that you may know how you ought to answer each one (Colossians 4:5-6).

It takes faith to boldly and directly challenge your audience. It also entails a degree of risk. As we relate to others and have those conversations surrounding spiritual matters, may the Lord Jesus guide us and be glorified through us as we share the "truth that sets men free" (John 8:32).

Heavenly Father, I acknowledge that being bold and direct in conversation is a challenging aspect of being a witness for you. Lord, I acknowledge my complete and utter dependence upon You in this matter. Please grant me wisdom, grace, and love to boldly and directly challenge others with truth according to Your time, in Your will, and for Your glory. Amen.

Always Be Ready (Acts 25:1–26:32)

Nervousness filled my being. I had one shot to get this right. There would be no do-over, no replay, no second chance. The one question that raced through my mind was, "Am I ready?"

It was my senior project in a Television/Radio Broadcasting course at the University of Florida. I was a telecommunications major. Our project team was presenting a start-up proposal for a new television station to a group of actual broadcast professionals. There was no fudging, faking, or flaking—these people were for real.

My job was to sell them on our hire for the Sales Manager position; his qualifications, his fit. Although I only had about two minutes for my portion of the presentation, I wanted to nail it. I wrote and memorized my talk. Wanting to get every word right, I practiced the delivery again and again. I did not want to wilt under pressure.

It was "go time" and all eyes were on me. It was my turn to present. I was on.

The fourth and final encounter we're tracking with Paul is his witness before King Agrippa in Acts 26. And it is here we touch upon one more principle to bolster our witness:

The setting (Acts 25:1-26). Two years had passed since Felix,

Governor of Judea first heard Paul. Felix was then succeeded by Festus, a member of the Roman nobility. Paul was still in prison. Before Festus and the Roman tribunal, Paul declares his right as a Roman citizen to have a trial in Rome before Caesar (Nero).

Festus grants Paul the request, but before going, Festus transfers the case to King Herod Agrippa II. Interestingly, one of the reasons Festus has Agrippa hear Paul is because he found Paul had "committed nothing worthy of death" and needed some kind of charge before sending a prisoner to Caesar (Acts 25:24-27).

The testimony (Acts 26:1-23). When Agrippa permitted Paul to speak, the apostle gave his testimony, his longest in the book of Acts. He shares about his early life prior to his conversion (Acts 26:1-11), recounts his conversion (Acts 26:12-18), and discusses his post-conversion ministry of proclaiming the gospel (Acts 26:19-23).

Paul is certainly ready to give a defense when called upon, displaying grace under pressure.

His witness epitomizes 1 Peter 3:15, which states:

> But in your hearts revere Christ as Lord. Always be prepared to give an answer to everyone who asks you to give the reason for the hope that you have. But do this with gentleness and respect.

Paul's gentleness and respect is illustrated in Acts 26:3 when he says to Agrippa, "I beg you to listen to me patiently."

Testifying about the Lord is not only about what we say, it's also about the spirit in which we say it.

Paul clearly shared the gospel, pointing out his charge to proclaim "light both to the Jewish people and the Gentiles" (Acts 26:23). His testimony evokes a powerful response.

The Reaction (Acts 26:24-32). Festus exclaimed in verse 24, "Paul you are out of your mind. Your great learning is driving you mad." Agrippa amazingly responds to the Apostle in verse 28, "In a short time you will persuade me to become a Christian."

Finally, we see the heart of Paul revealed as he responds to the King's comment:

"I would to God that not only you, but also all who hear me today, might become both almost and altogether such as I am, except for these chains" (Acts 26:29 italics mine). (See also 2 Corinthians 5:20.) Although in physical chains, Paul was free (John 8:32). And he wanted all people to know this freedom (John 8:36), including Festus and Agrippa. Upon conferring, they agree Paul had not done "anything worthy of death or imprisonment" (Acts 26:31). Despite that, Paul is still sent to Rome.

What does it mean to "always be ready?" Readiness is a lifestyle. To always be ready requires intentionality—an intentional desire to reflect the glory of God in word and in deed. Intentionality in practical terms also includes praying, studying God's Word, learning from others and from your own experiences, along with trial and error. As we daily abide in Christ, He will, through the power of the Holy Spirit, give us a "word aptly spoken" as He opens doors of opportunity.

Following the Lord and furthering the gospel had become central to Paul's life. And this foundation was a key to his readiness. He is a shining example to you and me.

A postscript. How did my broadcasting presentation I referred to earlier go? I nailed it. It felt good. Although our group didn't win the proposal, we did well for ourselves. I had done my part. And preparation was the key. When it was time to be "on" I was ready.

An interesting thing about the Christian life is this: we're always on. Why? Because being a witness for Jesus isn't just about Sunday mornings, it's about our daily walk with Christ.

Don't worry about what you will say if put in a position to give testimony under trial. The Lord will meet you at your point of need: "But when they deliver you up, do not worry about how or what you should speak. For it will be given to you in that hour what you should speak" (Matthew 10:19).

If the Lord met Paul at his need to give testimony under trial, he'll meet you at your need. And if under duress, how much more will He meet your need to be ready with a testimony in your daily affairs.

And God is faithful.

Chapter 12

Out Of The Doldrums And Into The Gale

The doldrums are regions of the Atlantic and Pacific oceans that have little if any wind. These constitute a unique environment on the earth. Located a little north of the equator, the doldrums effects can be felt from five degrees north of the equator to five degrees south of it.

The doldrums are caused by solar radiation, as sunlight beams down directly on the area around the equator. This heating causes the air to warm and rise straight up rather than blow horizontally. The result is little or no wind, sometimes for weeks on end.

One would think the doldrums favorable to maritime travel, but this hasn't always been the case. In fact, this was a particular problem for sailors, who in the past depended on the winds to propel their ships, a problem that could be potentially deadly.

Interestingly, while the prevailing wind in the doldrums is generally calm, the rising moist air in the region can also spawn squalls, sudden, sharp increase in wind speed usually associated with active weather like thunderstorms, severe thunderstorms, and even hurricanes. Nearly every Atlantic hurricane arises in or near the doldrums. The unpredictability of the weather, either no winds or potential hurricanes, made the doldrums one of the least favorite sailing lanes back when all that ships had to power them across the ocean was the wind in their sails.

The term appears to have arisen in the eighteenth century, when cross-equator sailing voyages became more common. The doldrums, noted for calm periods when the winds disappear altogether, was known for trapping sail-powered boats for periods of days or weeks.

As we conclude our thoughts on the rising gale of persecution against the church in recent decades and the continuing cultural blowback against the faith today, it's apparent our prevailing cultural drift away from God will continue.

The consequence for the American church is we need to learn to function within a new cultural paradigm. As culture drifts away from our Judeo-Christian foundation, our religious freedoms are being challenged and opposed, for the purpose of silencing our witness and keeping our faith in the closet.

The religious freedoms the American church may have taken for granted throughout much of our history were part of the spiritual doldrums or calm we experienced. Today we can say that we now have experienced a spiritual change, where the forecast appears ominous. We have moved out of the doldrums and into the gale. And the tempest doesn't seem that it will change any time soon, apart from an incredible work of God in our land.

But we've spent much time noting that our first century brethren functioned just fine amidst the gale of persecution.

The word "doldrums" colloquially means a state of inactivity, mild depression, listlessness, or stagnation. Is it possible that the rising winds of change making the expression of our faith more challenging may not be such a bad thing?

It seems American believers have a great opportunity to spiritually awaken to new awareness, become more lively about the Great Commission, and grow more concerned for the lost. We have been and continue to move out of the doldrums and into the gale. And as we've noted from one wise sage, "We don't choose our reality. We choose to enter our reality."

The New Normal

When cataclysmic meteorological events occur, like a Hurricane Harvey or Superstorm Sandy, cities like Houston or regions like the Jersey shore don't simply return to business as usual in a matter of months or sometimes even years.

In fact, as I strike the keyboard and as you read these words, the recovery continues. In many ways, those places will never be the same as they once were. But that's okay. They don't have a choice. "Rebuild", "renew", "restore" are catchwords of the day.

At the same time, structures have been rebuilt. The new normal is in place, because some of what was in place prior to those incredible events occurring has been destroyed, never to return quite like it was. Different, yes. And even in some ways, better.

For our purposes, the "new normal" is the cultural reality we find ourselves in today. And our country and culture didn't get here in just a few years. It's taken decades. It just appears to be accelerating in the wrong direction, away from the things of God. For example, do I think Bible reading and prayer will be re-introduced into public schools as the law of the land anytime soon? No.

But that's okay. We as His people still have the Word of God and prayer.

However the new normal may appear, there are some things that remain the same. Things transcendent, eternal, relevant to us today and tomorrow no matter the movement of our culture.

We are still called to be witnesses for Jesus. We still have the same power of God to do all He calls us to do. We still have the help and guidance of the Holy Spirit. And our Great Commission mandate remains:

> And Jesus came and spoke to them, saying, "All authority has been given to Me in heaven and on earth. Go therefore and make disciples of all the nations, baptizing them in the name of the Father and of the Son and of the Holy Spirit, teaching them to observe all things that I have commanded you; and lo, I am with you always, even to the end of the age." Amen (Matthew 28:18-20).

Additionally, our calling as God's people to be ministers of reconciliation is also a constant:

Therefore, if anyone is in Christ, he is a new creation; old things have passed away; behold, all things have become new. Now all things are of God, who has reconciled us to Himself through Jesus Christ, and has given us the ministry of reconciliation, that is, that God was in Christ reconciling the world to Himself, not imputing their trespasses to them, and has committed to us the word of reconciliation.

Now then, we are ambassadors for Christ, as though God were pleading through us: we implore you on Christ's behalf, be reconciled to God. For He made Him who knew no sin to be sin for us, that we might become the righteousness of God in Him" (2 Corinthians 5:17-21).

And lastly, God's love for humanity and his desire that people everywhere be saved remains constant, as He "is longsuffering toward us, not willing that any should perish but that all should come to repentance" (2 Peter 3:9).

"For God so loved the world that He gave His only begotten Son, that whoever believes in Him should not perish but have everlasting life" (John 3:16).

Yes, some things change, like culture, resulting in a new normal. Yet, some things remain the same, like God's plans and His promises.

What If It Gets Worse?

It's true, things may get worse, but God's faithfulness remains the same.

> God is our refuge and strength,
> A very present help in trouble.
> Therefore we will not fear,
> Even though the earth be removed,
> And though the mountains be carried into the midst of the sea;
> Though its waters roar and be troubled,
> Though the mountains shake with its swelling.
>
> There is a river whose streams shall make glad the city of God,
> The holy place of the tabernacle of the Most High.

God is in the midst of her, she shall not be moved;
God shall help her, just at the break of dawn.
The nations raged, the kingdoms were moved;
He uttered His voice, the earth melted.

The Lord of hosts is with us;
The God of Jacob is our refuge.

Come, behold the works of the LORD,
Who has made desolations in the earth.
He makes wars cease to the end of the earth;
He breaks the bow and cuts the spear in two;
He burns the chariot in the fire.

Be still, and know that I am God;
I will be exalted among the nations,
I will be exalted in the earth.

The LORD of hosts is with us;
The God of Jacob is our refuge. (Psalm 46)

Ultimately, Jesus will return and when He does, He will judge the world in righteousness and will right all wrongs. Justice will be served. In the interim, we must continue to proclaim His salvation not only in our wonderful country, but to the ends of the earth:

Oh, sing to the Lord a new song.
Sing to the Lord, all the earth.
Sing to the Lord, bless His name;
Proclaim the good news of His salvation from day to day.
Declare His glory among the nations,
His wonders among all peoples.

Say among the nations, "The Lord reigns;
The world also is firmly established,
It shall not be moved;
He shall judge the peoples righteously."

Let the heavens rejoice, and let the earth be glad;
Let the sea roar, and all its fullness;
Let the field be joyful, and all that is in it.
Then all the trees of the woods will rejoice before the Lord.
For He is coming, for He is coming to judge the earth.
He shall judge the world with righteousness,
And the peoples with His truth" (Psalm 96:1-3, 10-13).

Faithfulness To The End

The Apostle Paul knew well this commitment to follow Jesus was not a seasonal deployment, but rather a life-long endeavor. And no matter the season or circumstance, he remained resolute in fulfilling that commitment.

We see a terrific example of his determination to fulfill his service to the Lord while in a Roman prison in Acts 28, the final chapter in that remarkable book of the Bible.

While the book of Acts reveals the birth, growth, and expansion of the early church, it's interesting to note the final verses of Acts pertain to an individual believer, namely Paul. And therein lies an important lesson for you and for me.

As Paul enters house arrest in Acts 28, during his first of two Roman imprisonments, he was given the freedom to receive visitors. And who do you think he requested to visit?

It was Paul's usual ministry pattern to visit a synagogue upon entering a city or town. But since he was under house arrest, he invited the "leading men of the Jews" (Acts 28:17)—the most important men of the Rome synagogue, to visit him.

In Acts 28:17-22 Paul initially denies any transgression against the Jewish people, noting that he was "wearing this chain for the sake of the hope of Israel."

Sometime later, Paul receives a mixed response from the audience:

> So when they had appointed him a day, many came to him at his lodging, to whom he explained and solemnly testified of the kingdom of God, persuading them concerning Jesus from both

the Law of Moses and the Prophets, from morning till evening. And some were persuaded by the things which were spoken, and some disbelieved (Acts 28:23-24).

And it's not just immediately after arriving in Rome when Paul preached the gospel. He continues throughout his imprisonment:

> And he stayed two full years in his own rented quarters and was welcoming all who came to him, preaching the kingdom of God and teaching concerning the Lord Jesus Christ with all openness, unhindered (Acts 28:30-31).

Amazing. Paul evangelizes Rome for two years while under arrest. I'm inspired by the fact that Paul was "unhindered" in his ministry effort. Now you could say the Lord opened the door for Paul to preach and teach unhindered, and you would be right. Certainly the Roman government could have kept him in solitary confinement or prohibited visitors.

We see a great example of Paul's desire to be salt and light no matter the circumstance or season of life. Perhaps that's why, during his second Roman imprisonment, Paul anticipated his own martyrdom and encouraged his apprentice Timothy with these words: "Preach the word! Be ready in season and out of season. Convince, rebuke, exhort, with all longsuffering and teaching" (2 Timothy 4:2).

Nothing New Under The Sun

Earlier Paul provided context for this admonition, exhorting Timothy to remain faithful to fulfill his pastoral responsibilities. Perilous times and perilous men would certainly pose a great challenge and potential hindrance to Timothy:

> "But know this, that in the last days perilous times will come: For men will be lovers of themselves, lovers of money, boasters, proud, blasphemers, disobedient to parents, unthankful, unholy, unloving, unforgiving, slanderers, without self-control, brutal, despisers of good, traitors, headstrong,

haughty, lovers of pleasure rather than lovers of God, having a form of godliness but denying its power. And from such people turn away." (2 Timothy 3:1-5)

Those words, although penned over 2000 years ago, sure sound a lot like twenty-first century America. How powerful the prophetic word of God is. Today, you and I are living in perilous times amidst a corrupt and perverse generation. And we face our own potential hindrances in being the witnesses God calls us to be. Some of our potential hindrances today include, as we've mentioned, demands on personal time, political correctness, along with cultural barriers like post-modernism, cynicism, and skepticism.

For the follower of Jesus, being His witness in season and out of season means there is no offseason. Because in this season of life, we can regularly pray for the lost and for those witnessing to them (Matthew 9:37-38). We can also be intentional in developing friendships with people. We can serve people. And we can proclaim truth as God opens doors of opportunity.

Paul ministered the gospel while in prison and when he was free. His commitment to serve the Lord and be a witness even amidst challenges, difficulties and trials is exemplary.

Today, may we be inspired by Paul's exemplary witness as we follow Jesus in whatever season of life we find ourselves. People need the Lord...in season and out of season. And as we do this work, may we take these words to heart and strive to follow the Lord with the days He has left for us to live: "I have fought the good fight, I have finished the race, I have kept the faith" (2 Timothy 4:7).

Keep Our Eyes On Jesus

We conclude our study focusing on the Lord Himself, our Rock, our Redeemer, and the author and finisher of our faith:

> Therefore we also, since we are surrounded by so great a cloud of witnesses, let us lay aside every weight, and the sin which so easily ensnares us, and let us run with endurance the race that is set before us, looking unto Jesus, the author and finisher of

our faith, who for the joy that was set before Him endured the cross, despising the shame, and has sat down at the right hand of the throne of God. For consider Him who endured such hostility from sinners against Himself, lest you become weary and discouraged in your souls (Hebrews 12:1-3).

Meditate upon those inspired words. Lay aside sin. Run the race with endurance. Look unto Jesus. Consider His suffering and persecution, so you won't become weary and discouraged.

Keeping our eyes on Jesus amidst the storms is crucial. Peter learned this in the middle of a physical storm:

> Immediately Jesus made His disciples get into the boat and go before Him to the other side, while He sent the multitudes away. And when He had sent the multitudes away, He went up on the mountain by Himself to pray. Now when evening came, He was alone there. But the boat was now in the middle of the sea, tossed by the waves, for the wind was contrary.
>
> Now in the fourth watch of the night Jesus went to them, walking on the sea. And when the disciples saw Him walking on the sea, they were troubled, saying, "It is a ghost." And they cried out for fear. But immediately Jesus spoke to them, saying, "Be of good cheer. It is I; do not be afraid." And Peter answered Him and said, "Lord, if it is You, command me to come to You on the water." So He said, "Come." And when Peter had come down out of the boat, he walked on the water to go to Jesus (Matthew 14:22-29).

In the storm, the Lord beckoned Peter to take a step of faith and exit the boat. When Peter does get out of the boat, he walked on water. So far, so good. Then He took His eyes off Jesus.

> But when he saw that the wind was boisterous, he was afraid; and beginning to sink he cried out, saying, "Lord, save me." And immediately Jesus stretched out His hand and caught him, and said to him, "O you of little faith, why did you doubt?" And when they got into the boat, the wind ceased.

Then those who were in the boat came and worshiped Him, saying, "Truly You are the Son of God" (Matthew 14:29-33).

When Peter took His eyes off Jesus, he got into trouble. The beautiful thing is this: Jesus never took His eyes off Peter. Again, God is faithful.

No matter the storms you and I are facing or will face, the Lord is with us. He never leaves us nor forsakes us. The winds of trouble this life brings will end soon, whether Jesus returns for us or we go to Him.

And forever we will, with all the saints, worship Him, saying, "You are the Son of God." Amen.

"For it was fitting for Him, for whom are all things and by whom are all things, in bringing many sons to glory, to make the captain of their salvation perfect through sufferings" (Hebrews 2:10).

About The Author

Christianity Is Jewish!

I know, I know! I'm stating the obvious! Or perhaps that's a revelation to you. Whatever your response to that statement, know that my views about that statement have changed dramatically. At one point it was completely irrelevant. Today, that comment plays a major role in who I am as a human being.

Growing up in a Reform Jewish home in St. Pete, Florida, I attended synagogue, and at age thirteen went through Bar-Mitzvah which means "son of the commandment" and is a ceremonial rite of passage when a Jewish boy becomes a man. Though we were culturally and socially very connected to the Jewish community, we were not a particularly religious household.

Growing up, I believed in God as far back as I can remember and had some sense that He knew me. In high school I sought fulfillment in athletics and academics, as I was a state-ranked tennis player in Florida and an honors student. But accomplishment didn't fulfill the longings of my soul.

In college at the University of Florida I got involved in the party scene. This didn't satisfy me either. In fact, I was that young person walking in quiet desperation—empty and walking without a plan for life.

My earliest memories of people sharing Jesus with me go back to my college years. But, I consistently rejected any conversation about Jesus and turned down invitations to church,

Bible studies, and Christian concerts. Then a good friend, Greg, a Christian, challenged me. He said, "Do you know who you are and do you know where you're going when you die?" I had no idea how to answer those questions. In fact, they sent me into an existential crisis of sorts. God used that crisis as a catalyst, as I began searching for truth in 1985.

At that time, I embraced neither my Judaism nor any other religion, but began to examine different philosophies and world religions for answers to life's biggest questions.

I searched for something I could believe in, something that would fill a void I felt in my life that accomplishment or earthly pleasures could not fill. My search culminated in the fall of 1987 when a stranger on a plane challenged me to ask the God of Israel if Jesus is the Messiah. I took his challenge, crying out to God as I knew Him to show me the truth about Jesus.

He did, and in December 1987 I trusted in Jesus. I believed for the first time that He died for my sins and rose again from the dead so that I could be forgiven. Knowing Messiah was and is the greatest thing that's ever happened in my life, but it's not easy being a Jew for Jesus.

Something profound occurred in my life as a new Christian: I made a discovery that was quite astonishing to me at the time. As I began studying the New Testament, I learned about the Jewishness of Jesus. I also learned all the writers of the New Testament were Jewish with the possible exception of Luke. I thought to myself, "Christianity is Jewish!"

In one sense the gospel narrative is simply a Jewish debate among Jewish people about the true identity of a Jewish man, Jesus. And the story takes place in Israel. What could be more Jewish than that?

The Impact Of The Holocaust

My father and his family immigrated from Bonn, Germany in June 1939, escaping Nazi persecution. My paternal grandparents and my young father escaped with help from an SS Agent in the Nazi party. The agent, a friend of my grandfather's from WWI, falsified immigration papers enabling my father and his parents to escape to Belize, where they lived for two years before moving to Daytona Beach in 1941. None of my father's remaining family in Germany survived the holocaust.

Professional Tennis Coaching

I picked up my first tennis racquet at the age of 9 and from the ages of 12 to 18 I competed in the Florida junior circuit, earning my highest state ranking of #20 in the boys 16-under singles division. It was my main sport, though I loved playing many sports. After graduating from the University of Florida in 1986, I began coaching under my high school coach, Billy Stearns, at his academy in Seminole, Florida. I trained world-class juniors, college and professional tennis players. During my 20s and 30s, I was a professional tennis coach who loved my outdoor "office" and working with people. I came to East Tennessee to pursue my Master's Degree in 1991, and joined the coaching staff at East Tennessee State University under Head Coach Dave Mullins. Coach and I worked together for nine years, and I taught private lessons and clinics on the side with a faithful client base.

Stepping Away From The Racquet

As I grew as a Christian, my desire to share this good news with my Jewish people also grew. I wanted them to know that yes, it is Jewish to believe in Jesus, for He is the Jewish Messiah and Savior of the world. I prayed for God to make an opportunity for me to share the gospel with fellow Jews.

In 1989 a family friend passed on a pamphlet from Jews for Jesus, a missionary society committed to sharing Messiah with the Jewish people. Before receiving this newsletter I thought I was alone, the only Jew who believed in Jesus.

After a few years of receiving the newsletter, I decided to serve for a six-week summer outreach with Jews for Jesus. In the process of applying, I learned about The Liberated Wailing Wall, Jews for Jesus' mobile evangelistic music team. This team shared the good news of Jesus through music, drama, and testimony, mainly at churches and at Christian colleges. They also would engage in street evangelism in big cities and on college campuses. After much consideration and prayer, I went ahead and applied for the music team as well.

In the plan of God, a six-week short-term mission trip turned into a two-year full-time ministry commitment. In June of 1997, I left Johnson City, Tennessee with no more than a book bag, a twenty-nine–inch hard-shell suitcase, and a guitar. Everything else I left in storage. I boarded an airplane, flew away and entered a life-changing adventure!

In December of 1997, before my team left for our tour of ministry, we recorded a messianic praise album called, *This is Jerusalem*.

In January 1998, my team of six members and I loaded our gear onto a forty-foot fully-equipped tour bus, which became our home on the road. I co-led the traveling music team on our journey around the United States and Canada from January 1998 to March 1999. At the end of our North American tour, we embarked on a two-month world tour doing ministry in England, South Africa, Australia, and Hawaii.

Needless to say, after doing over 500 presentations in a myriad of diverse church settings and evangelizing around the world, my life was forever changed.

During my tour, I courted a beautiful woman named Lori, and at the end of the tour I asked her to be my wife. We were married in the fall of 1999 and two years later God blessed us with our firstborn son, Elijah.

Ministry In The Big Apple

In 2002, I was accepted onto vocational missionary staff with Jews for Jesus. My family and I packed up our house and moved to New York City in January of 2003. Arriving in the Big Apple, we moved into our apartment in midtown Manhattan. Shortly after arriving in New York City, Lori and I learned that we were expecting our second child, a daughter.

In Manhattan, I trained under some of the brightest and most gifted missionaries and Bible teachers including the late Dr. Jhan Moskowitz, who taught me much about preaching, and Dr. Jack Meadows, my private theology professor. Following the training, I was ordained, and then continued on as a missionary in the heart of New York City through mid-2009.

Pastoral Service

Grace Fellowship in Johnson City, TN has been the most influential church in my Christian life. It was there I learned to function in a local body of believers. The church supported and sent me out on both my two-year and six-year missionary stints with Jews for Jesus. Just prior to leaving for New York City in January 2003, I sat under staff pastor Tim Bowers in a six month resident's program where my main responsibilities included developing a seeker-sensitive, gospel-centered Bible study.

After leaving staff with Jews for Jesus in 2009, I served as Missionary-in-Residence for a year before becoming the full-time

Local Outreach Pastor. During my service at Grace Fellowship from 2009-2013, I developed and directed various community outreach programs and mission activities, trained missions teams, taught classes and preached on a number of occasions.

Larry Stamm Ministries

I am a Jewish Christian in love with Jesus the Messiah and the Word of God. God's work in my life to this point prepared me to launch Larry Stamm Ministries in early 2013 with the full support of our Board of Directors, my family, and my home church. My experience since 1997 in witnessing around the globe to people of all walks of life has uniquely qualified me to teach and share biblical principles with others and to help them share their faith more confidently.

More and more Americans are avoiding the church and an increasing number of both irreligious and religiously unaffiliated no longer have friends who are Christians. We can't afford to isolate ourselves, or to stop reaching out to our co-workers, neighbors, classmates, and others. The onus is ever more upon individual Christians to share Jesus in the marketplace: at the coffee shop, with your neighbor or coworker, your classmates and others with whom you have everyday contact.

Larry Stamm Ministries exists to make the gospel of Jesus a confident topic of conversation for every Christian. We provide classes, one-on-one evangelism coaching and teaching that connects the dots between the Old and New Testaments to inspire Christians to press on in fulfilling the Great Commission.

Connect With Larry

Larry Stamm Ministries
Post Office Box 1072
Jonesborough, TN 37659

Phone: 423-426-5055

E-mail: lsm@larrystamm.org

Twitter: https://twitter.com/LarryStamm

Facebook: https://www.facebook.com/larrystamm.org

Author website: http://larrystamm.org/

Vimeo Video Channel:
https://vimeo.com/channels/larrystammministries

Endnotes

[1] Paul Nyquist, *Prepare: Living Your faith in an Increasingly Hostile Culture*, (Chicago: Moody Publishers, 2015), 16.

[2] Nyquist, *Prepare—Living Your Faith in an Increasingly Hostile Culture*, 16.

[3] Francis A. Schaefer, *How Then Shall We Live: The Rise and Decline of Western Thought and Culture*, (Old Tappan, NJ: Fleming H. Revell, 1976) From the title.

[4] Ifte Choudhury, "Cultural Definition," Texas A & M faculty website, quoted from *Prepare: Living Your Faith In An Increasingly Hostile Culture* by J. Paul Nyquist, 43.

[5] James Emory, "Are Christians In America Under Attack?" by christianity.com—whitehttp://www.christianity.com/christian-life/political-and-social-issues/are-christians-in-america-under-attack.html, October, 2012

[6] Jonah Goldberg, "Liberals are the True Aggressors in Culture Wars," *USA Today,* (February 6, 2012).

[7] Wind Energy Foundation Online, http://windenergyfoundation.org/about-wind-energy/history/

[8] https://en.wikipedia.org/wiki/Wind_turbine

[9] Wind Energy Foundation Online, http://windenergyfoundation.org/about-wind-energy/how-wind-works/

[10] https://en.wikipedia.org/wiki/Volvo_Ocean_Race

[11] http://www.volvooceanrace.com/en/the-race/12_Volvo-Ocean-Race-Trophy.html

[12] https://en.wikipedia.org/wiki/Volvo_Ocean_Race

[13] David Pratt, http://www.beliefnet.com/columnists/news/2013/09/are-denominations-dividing-the-church.php

[14] *Ecumenical Creeds and Reformed Confessions,* (Grand Rapids: Board of Publications of the Christian Reformed Church, 1979), 3.

[15] http://www.ligonier.org/learn/articles/essentials-unity-non-essentials-liberty-all-things/

[16] Norman Geisler and Ron Rhodes, *Conviction Without Compromise: Standing Strong in the Core Beliefs of the Christian Faith,* (Eugene, OR: Harvest House Publishers, 2008), Taken from table of contents

[17] Mark Howell, *Exalting Jesus in 1st & 2nd Thessalonians,* (Nashville: B&H Publishing Group, 2015), 21.

[18] Mathew Henry, *Matthew Henry Online Bible Commentary,* John 17:20–21, https://www.biblestudytools.com/commentaries/matthew-henry-complete/john/17.html

[19] Kate Ravilious, April 14, 2013 online edition of The Guardian, https://www.theguardian.com/news/2013/apr/14/weather-fronts-maps

[20] Bellamy, Francis, "The Story of the Pledge of Allegiance to the Flag," University of Rochester Library Bulletin, Vol. VIII, Winter 1953. http://rbscp.lib.rochester.edu/3418

[21] http://www.ushistory.org/documents/pledge.htm

[22] Arron Chambers, *Eats With Sinners,* (Cincinnati: Standard Publishing, 2009), 14.

[23] Chambers, *Eats With Sinners,* 15.

[24] http://www.u-s-history.com/pages/h1854.html

[25] https://www.accuweather.com/en/weather-news/weather-played-a-role-in-great/38495

[26] http://www.cityclock.org/chicago-fire/#.WiIK0K2ZOt9

[27] https://www.ccel.org/ccel/schaff/anf03.iv.iii.l.html and http://thegoodheart.blogspot.com/2009/06/blood-of-christians-is-seed.html

[28] Dietrich Bonhoeffer, Eberhard Bethge ed., *Letters and Papers from Prison*, 2nd ed., (London: SCM Press Ltd., 1971), 369.

[29] James Emory White, "Hills to Die On," *Church & Culture Blog*, (July 20, 2017), http://www.churchandculture.org/Blog.asp?ID=11634

[30] http://blogs.lt.vt.edu/malw14/2015/11/16/andrei-sakharov/ OR *Time Magazine*, Feb. 21, 1977.

[31] James Emory White, *Online Church and Culture Blog*, "Meet the Nones," Oct. 15, 2012, http://www.churchandculture.org/Blog.asp?ID=3446

[32] Wayne's Word Blog, February 1999, http://www2.palomar.edu/users/warmstrong/plfeb99.htm

[33] Earl D. Radmacher, gen. ed, *The NKJV Study Bible*, (Wheaton, Tyndale, 2007), 1610, comment on Luke 8:11.

[34] Eric Swanson & Rick Rusaw, *The Externally Focused Quest: Becoming the Best Church for the Community* (San Francisco: John Wiley & Sons/, Jossey-Bass, 2010), 159.

[35] Swanson, Rusaw, *The Externally Focused Quest: Becoming the Best Church for the Community,* 159.

[36] Swanson, Rusaw, *Externally Focused Quest: Becoming the Best Church for the Community,* 160.

[37] Alvin Reid, *Introduction To Evangelism,* (Nashville: B&H Publishing Group, 1998), 140.

[38] Bill Bright, *Witnessing Without Fear: How to Share Your Faith with Confidence*, (Nashville: Thomas Nelson, 1993), 67.

[39] Dave Earley, David Wheeler, *Evangelism is...,* (Nashville: B&H Publishing Group, 2010), 14.

[40] Henry T. Blackaby & Claude V. King, *Experiencing God: How to Live the Full Adventure of Knowing and Doing the Will of God*, (Nashville: B&H Publishing Group, 2008), 148.

[41] Henry T. Blackaby, Tom Blackaby, *The Man God Uses*, (Nashville: B&H Publishing Group, 1999), 83.

[42] Henry Thoreau, *Walden: Life in the Woods*, (New York: Thomas Y. Crowell & Company, 1910), 119.